# Horsing Around Toronto and Beyond

# Horsing Around Toronto and Beyond

HELEN MASON

**WHITECAP BOOKS**
*Vancouver/Toronto*

Whitecap Books
Vancouver/Toronto



Edited by Linda Ostrowalker
Cover design by Warren Clark
Interior design by Susan Doering
Cover photograph by Adam Smith Productions/First Light
Interior photographs by Helen Mason and the Ontario Ministry of Agriculture and Food
Typeset by CryptoGraphics

Printed and bound in Canada

**Canadian Cataloguing in Publication Data**

Mason, Helen, 1950–
Horsing around Toronto and beyond

Includes index.
ISBN 1-55110-092-4

1. Horsemanship—Ontario, Southwestern—Guidebooks. 2. Trail Riding—Ontario, Southwestern—Guidebooks. I. Title.
SF309.257.C2M38 1993 798.2'3'09713 C93-091531-3

# Acknowledgements

I WOULD LIKE TO thank all the Ontario horseback riders and horse nuts who assisted me in finding the listings in this book, and the stable owners who took the time to provide the material I requested. Special thanks to staff at the Community Association for Riding for the Disabled, for putting me in touch with other stables that assist disabled riders. Thanks also to Pat Gottlieb, a dear friend, who has always supported my riding and writing projects.

*This book is dedicated to Chukka and The Bold One,*
*two special horses among all those with whom I have*
*spent thousands of pleasurable hours on the trails.*
*With special thanks to Pat Gottlieb, Audrey Steiner,*
*and Chris Rumney, with whom I have enjoyed many trails.*

# Table of Contents

# Introduction

HORSES. THE VERY WORD brings daydreams of velvet muzzles and hardy steeds, their manes flowing in the wind. Can such daydreams be realized if you're living in a city? They certainly can. Southern Ontario has a wide variety of riding opportunities that will delight all types of riders.

Did you know, for example, that Toronto area riding lesson stables include opportunities for those interested in both English and Western riding, as well as for those with intellectual, emotional, or physical disabilities? Did you know that Ontario has places where you can enjoy a moonlit ride far from the day-to-day noise of city traffic? And that these moonlight rides can end with a singsong around the campfire, a relaxing hot tub, or a glass of fragrant wine? All of these riding experiences can be enjoyed right here in Ontario—and a lot of it is within an easy drive of Toronto.

To help you find such opportunities, *Horsing Around Toronto and Beyond* is divided into four chapters:

**1. Trail Riding Stables.** This chapter includes places where you can take a horse for a pleasant trail ride in or close to Metro Toronto. The listings include the following information:

- Stable name, mailing address, and phone number.
- Name of contact person.
- Street location and access to public transit, if any.
- Stable hours or season.
- Type of rate structure the stable has. Due to the possibility of price changes, actual rates are not included. Prices can, however, vary from stable to stable. If price is a concern, phone around to do a price comparison.
- Age recommendation for riders.
- Outline of the type of facility, number and type of horses, style of saddle used, and whether or not helmets are available. Explanation of how beginning and novice riders are handled.
- A description of the terrain through which the trail ride passes.
- Any other special services the stable offers, including, when available, advice to experienced riders on how to get one of the stable's more challenging horses.

Using these listings, you can spend a cold winter evening or rainy summer afternoon dreaming of riding days to come.

**2. Riding Lesson Stables.** These include facilities where you can learn the basics of horsemanship in or close to Metro Toronto. The Lesson Stable listings include:

- Name, mailing address, and phone number.
- Name of person to contact regarding lessons.
- Location, and access to public transportation, if any.
- The types of lessons available.
- Type of rate structure the stable has. Due to the possibility of price changes, actual rates are not included.
- Age recommendation for riders.
- An outline of what riders are expected to wear.
- Outline of the facilities available for riders, including the number and types of lesson horses.
- Qualifications of riding instructors.

- The different kinds of lessons available (private, semiprivate, group), and the maximum number of riders in a group lesson.
- Availability of introductory packages for beginners.
- Availability of other special services such as boarding, horse leasing, Pony Club, facilities for people with disabilities, coaching on the show circuit, etc.

This information will help you choose a stable that provides the kind of riding instruction and amenities that appeal to your particular taste.

**3. Riding Adventures.** These include longer trail rides and riding packages more than an hour's drive from Metro Toronto. Many are exciting day tours or relaxing horse lover's holidays. Look here if you're planning that unforgettable birthday party, a weekend outing with a friend, or an exciting adventure tour of some of Canada's northland. Each of these listings include:

- Name, mailing address, and phone number.
- Person to contact regarding adventure tours.
- Location of facility.
- Season of operation.
- Rate information. Due to the possibility of price changes, actual rates are not included.
- Age recommendation for riders.
- Explanation of the type of riding facility and what riding opportunities are available. This includes the type of adventure, number of available horses, types of saddles used, and whether or not helmets are available.
- Outline of any introduction for beginners.
- Description of the type of terrain.
- Availability of other special services such as hay rides, sleigh rides, overnight camping, etc.

**4. Riding Camps.** This chapter is subdivided into two sections. First are the listings of riding day camps throughout Ontario. Second are the listings of residential camps that include everything from camps that have a once-a-week riding program to those designed almost exclusively around horse-related activities.

This chapter is for your favourite young rider. I grew up in the city where the closest I came to the steed of my dreams was the old horse that pulled the bread wagon from a nearby bakery. If your child is the type who reads every horse book in the local library, tapes pictures of assorted equines to the bedroom wall, and generally thinks that anything with four legs, a mane, and a tail is the most beautiful thing in the world, this is the chapter that will interest you the most. It provides listings of residential and day camps that offer riding experience for the complete novice. Each listing includes:

- Name, mailing address, and phone number of the camp office.
- The person to contact about camp offerings.
- Location of the camp.
- Season of operation.
- Rate information. Due to the possibility of price changes, actual rates are not included.
- Age recommendation for campers.
- A description of the camp program, including the types of lessons offered, size of groups, and a list of equine-related activities.
- Qualifications of instructors.
- Availability of other facilities such as related outdoor activities.

Let me encourage you to use this book to help you see Ontario the "ride" way. Don't be surprised if you find that there is no better way to enjoy this beautiful province—or any other.

CHAPTER ONE

# Trail Riding Stables in the Metro Toronto Area

YOU MAY BE SURPRISED to discover that there are riding stables right within the Toronto city limits. In fact, you can enjoy the Rouge Valley or even explore Claireville Conservation Area while riding rented horses. You can take a friend on a cozy spring ride, or enjoy a company picnic—either on horseback or with a hay ride thrown in. You can even take an overnight trail ride—all within an easy drive of Metro Toronto.

## RESERVATIONS

Now that your appetite is whetted, plan ahead. Most stables prefer that you call ahead for reservations. Some will even give reductions to those who do. Others provide discounts for people who take the time to organize a riding group.

Know your limitations before making the reservations. For most beginners—especially those who are not physically fit—a one-hour ride is plenty. Even experienced riders build up to longer sessions.

## RIDING APPAREL

Safety in horseback riding includes dressing appropriately. Leave the designer clothes, stylish hairdos, and flimsy footwear at home. Instead, wear sturdy washable clothes. Give your pants this riding once-over:

> Can you do a deep knee bend without your pants binding at the hips or knees?
> Standing upright, can you bend your knee, grab it with one hand, and bring it towards your chest without straining the fabric?

If you cannot do both of these exercises with ease, the pants are too tight. Doing the test several times is also a good pre-ride exercise.

How thick are your pants? Many cowboys use denim, a material thick enough to protect them from the wear and tear of many hours in the saddle. If your denim jeans aren't loose enough to pass the above riding test, consider wearing long underwear, tights, or even nylons beneath a thinner pair of slacks. Like a second pair of socks in cross-country ski boots, these will eliminate a lot of potentially painful skin rubbing.

You might also consider tucking the ends of your jeans into a pair of long socks. If you don't, and your pant legs ride up, you may get a painful blister where your bare leg rubs against the saddle or stirrup leathers.

The best riding stables won't let you on a horse without a helmet. That's because head injuries are the most common serious injuries associated with horses. This doesn't mean that you need to buy an expensive felt-covered riding helmet. Many recreational riders use hockey, bicycle, skating, motorcycle, or snowmobile helmets. These may not be as flashy as riding helmets, but they are effective.

Around horses, it's also important to protect your feet from two major problems. Some horses with an equine sense of humour love to casually stomp on a novice rider's foot. To protect your feet from such pranksters, try steel-toed construction boots, or hiking or rubber boots with a thickly padded toe area. This, coupled with a sharp slap to the belly (of the horse), and a growling, "Quit," will discourage many foot stompers. Even better, keep an eye on those horses' feet and try to stay out of range.

The second problem with feet is the stirrups. Once you're on the horse, your feet will be supported in wooden or iron stirrups. To prevent your feet from slipping too far into the stirrups, you'll need shoes or boots with a heel. The ideal boot comes above the ankle. This serves both to support and protect your lower leg from the stirrup leathers, which can rub against and bruise exposed skin. Don't worry about wearing anything fancy. Rubber rain boots or winter boots without zippers are both suitable. Don't use winter boots with a zipper on the inside of your leg as it may rub you raw and will certainly scratch the saddle you're using.

## HORSE TACK

Horse tack or equipment comes in two types. Western tack is the kind used by cowboys. Its major advantage is a horn on the saddle that was originally designed for roping cattle, but conveniently doubles as a safety handle for beginning riders with a touchy sense of balance.

Many experienced riders prefer the closeness and comfort of an English saddle, which is smaller, flatter, and does not have a horn. If you ride with an English saddle, remember that the horse won't get mad if you grab a handful of mane to help maintain your balance.

## TRAIL RIDING ETIQUETTE

Always remember that the trail guide's word is law. The guide has been chosen because of his (or her) experience with horses. Listening to what he says, and watching what he does, is about as good as any riding lesson. It's also the safest way to enjoy your ride.

On most trail rides, the horses are put into position based on the horses' pecking order. Within the pecking order, some horses can boss other horses without getting bossed back. It also means that some horses will travel in front of or behind certain other horses without a problem; but, paired with a horse they don't like, will cause trouble. Riding stable owners keep their horses' likes and dislikes in mind when lining up their mounts for a trail ride. Especially for beginner riders, they put their horses in an order in which the horses feel the most comfortable—and are the safest. Leave them there.

## THE BASICS OF RIDING

Most riding stables will show you the basics of controlling your horse as soon as you mount up. If one doesn't, here are some very elementary instructions:

**1. Turning:** By holding one rein in each hand, turning becomes relatively simple. A gentle pull on the left rein means turn left. A gentle pull on the right rein means turn right. There are other methods or reining. Ask your trail guide for assistance if you need it.

**2. Slowing and Stopping:** Most horses are trained to stop when the rider pulls gently on both reins simultaneously and leans slightly back in the saddle.

**3. Forward Movement:** To ask a horse to move forward, squeeze it firmly with both legs, using your heels and/or your entire calf. Start gently. If the horse ignores your request, try a firm kick.

It can be difficult trying to balance yourself on a moving horse. That's why most trail rides are fairly slow. They start at a walk, and if the riders seem comfortable, the guide may ask if they would like to try a jog. A jog, which is a slow trot, can be a bit bumpy so be prepared to hold on. Relaxing your back muscles as you do when you're pumping a swing can help you stay in place.

Many trail rides, especially those with young children, won't go faster than a slow jog. With more experienced riders, the guide may allow the horses to lope or canter (the proper name for a slow run) along a short stretch. Some riders find it easier to lean slightly forward at this speed. Holding on to the saddle horn is not required but makes some people feel a lot safer.

If you're already an experienced trail riding fan, you probably know everything I've said so far—and more. You probably know, for example, that horses are creatures of habit. Horses that have been at a trail riding stable for a period of time will always follow behind the horse in front, no matter what the rider is trying to tell them. This is great for inexperienced riders, but can be a little tedious for people who are used to guiding their own mount.

How do you get a horse with a bit of a challenge? Most riding stables do have some less passive horses, but they're often the ones used by the guides. Unfortunately for the experienced rider, few reputable stables will offer you one of the lead horses, or let you take a horse out on your own the first time out. The problem is two-fold. First, there's liability. Stable owners are responsible for their customer's safety, and if something happens to one of their riders, they can be legally liable. That's why all riding stables pay high insurance premiums, and why they're very careful to make sure that you, the customer, have a safe ride.

Secondly, some inexperienced riders claim to be experts. In the trade they're often referred to as "weekend cowboys" or by other less complimentary terms. Usually it's pretty easy to tell the difference between these braggarts and the real horse people. The stable owner or guide simply watches how the customer moves around the horses and how the horses react to him or her.

If you really are a rider who has many years experience on the trail, has taken lessons, owned your own horse, or participated in other horse activities, let the stable owner or trail guide know. Once they see that you can handle a horse, they may offer you one of the stable's better mounts. If not, enjoy the ride the best you can and hope for a better horse next time. If you really know your stuff, you'll likely get one.

## CHILDREN AND TRAIL RIDING

Many trail riding stables won't allow young children on the trail. Others allow children to ride double with their parents.

Since most experts agree that riding double is *not* a safe practice, I would recommend that you don't take children trail riding unless they are tall enough for their feet to fit into the stirrups of the saddle they're using. Even then, make sure that the trail guides have experience with young beginners and won't let them go faster than they can handle. Usually this means a walk and slow trot or jog.

If a young child insists on riding, consider looking for private lessons with a competent instructor, or look for places where you can rent a pony you lead around an enclosed paddock. There are several such places close to Metro Toronto.

## TRAIL RIDING STABLE LISTINGS

### *Within Metro Toronto*

**Claireville Ranch**
P.O. Box 1082, Station C
Rexdale, ON M9V 2B3
Phone: (905) 794-0700

**Contact:** Barb Newland, or whoever answers the phone.
**Location:** Highway 7, approximately three kilometres west of Highway 427, on Claireville Conservation Road, which runs south of Highway 7. Take the Brampton bus along Highway 7.
**Open:** Year-round. Open six days per week April to October. Closed Tuesdays. Spring and fall hours are Monday to Friday, 1:00 p.m. to dark; Saturday, Sunday, and holidays, 10:00 a.m. to dusk. Open 2:00 p.m. to dark during July and August. Winter hours: weekends only, 12:00 noon to 4:00 p.m.
**Rates:** Hourly; special rate for pancake breakfast and ride; hay rides and snack by arrangement; members of the stable riding club get discount rates.
**Age Recommendations:** Ten and up on the trail. Children nine and under ride ponies that parents lead around an enclosure. Some nine-year-olds may ride on the trail if they are tall enough

for their feet to reach the stirrups.
**Facilities and Services:** Trail riding. Guided tours through the conservation area. Western. The stable riding club offers a two-hour trail ride every Saturday, overnight camping, breakfast rides, and parties. Twenty-five to thirty horses, many of Pinto, Appaloosa, and draft breeding. Some ponies.
**Terrain:** Forest, hills, streams. Riders frequently see deer, rabbits, and Great Blue Herons.
**Other Services:**

- Riding lessons (see listing in Chapter 2).
- One or two horse shows per year.
- Riders with CEF Rider Level 2 qualifications may ride without a guide if they are with another rider of the same level.

**Rouge Hill Riding Centre**
1885 Rosefield Road
Pickering, ON L1Y 1A2
Phone: (416) 284-6176

**Location:** .5 kilometres east of Port Union Road on Highway 2. Take the Rouge Hill #13 bus from Rouge Hill GO Station or at Meadowvale and Shepherd.
**Open:** Year-round. Summer hours: 10:00 a.m. to 4:15 p.m. Monday to Friday; 8:00 a.m. to 4:15 p.m. Saturdays and Sundays. Winter hours: 10:00 a.m. to 4:15 p.m. Monday to Friday; 8:45 a.m. to 4:15 p.m. on weekends.
**Rates:** Hourly, higher on holidays and Sunday afternoons; 1 1/2-hour evening ride; 1 1/2-hour 8:00 a.m. ride; breakfast ride.
**Age Recommendations:** Nine and up. Younger children can ride a pony led by an adult around a paddock.
**Facilities and Services:** Trail riding through the Rouge Valley. The stable has about twenty-two horses, including registered Quarter Horses, Appaloosas, Paints, and grade stock. Western saddles. Helmets are available and must be worn by children up to the age of sixteen.

Beginners receive basic instruction when they're put on the

horses. This includes instruction in how to turn and stop. All trail rides are supervised by one to three guides.
**Terrain:** The Rouge Valley is a large tract of public land where riders often see deer, fox, blue herons, and rabbits.
**Other Services:**

- Riding lessons (see listing in Chapter 2).
- Trail guides carry two-way radios for use in emergencies. Some guides have St. John's Ambulance Training.
- Corporate rides include a Friday evening ride, barbecue, and bonfire for large groups. Late April to Labour Day.
- School group rides can handle forty-five students who are rotated between trail riding, a mini lesson, and instruction in grooming and tack.
- Breakfast rides on holiday Mondays. $2^1/_2$-hour ride plus ranch breakfast.
- Regular clients who have passed a riding test receive a Green Card that allows them use the trails without supervision.

*North of Metro Toronto*

**Circle M**
P.O. Box 189
Woodbridge, ON L4L 1B1
Phone: (905) 851-0503

**Location:** On Highway 27, three kilometres north of Highway 7. One kilometre north of the last bus stop for the Woodbridge bus.
**Open:** April to end of November. Spring and fall hours: 10:00 a.m. to 6:00 p.m. Summer hours: 10:00 a.m. to 8:00 p.m.
**Rates:** Hourly.
**Age Recommendations:** Eight and up. Have very quiet horses suitable for youngsters and beginners.
**Facilities and Services:** Supervised trail rides. Most rides at a walk and slow trot or jog. Rides with more experienced riders will do some loping or slow cantering. The stable has approximately twenty-five Western-type Quarter Horses, Pintos,

Palominos, and grade stock. There is a variety of sizes from ponies to horses large enough to carry heavy riders. Western saddles. No helmets.

Trail guides explain how to sit on a horse, hold the reins, stop, and go. They warn riders to keep one horse length back from the horse in front and explain how to do it.

**Terrain:** 160 acres of field and creek.

**Other Services:**

- Regular clients who are experienced can choose their own mounts once the guides see they have the ability to ride and control a horse.

**Lionel's Pony Farm**
11714 McCowan Road
R.R. #2
Markham, ON L3P 3J3
Phone: (905) 640-PONY

**Location:** Just south of Stouffville Road on the west side of McCowan Road.

**Open:** Sundays and holidays from 12:00 noon to 5:00 p.m., Victoria Day to Thanksgiving.

**Rates:** Small fee for riding ponies.

**Facilities and Services:** Pony rides for children age ten and under. Western saddles. Ponies are led by a parent or guardian around the petting zoo.

**Other Services:**

- Free petting zoo with farm animals, llamas, miniature goats, donkeys, rabbits, and pheasants.
- Birthday parties, school tours, and senior citizen days.
- Hay wagon rides.

**Park Lane Ranch**
R.R. #2
Tottenham, ON L0G 1W0
Phone: (905) 936-2658

**Location:** 4th line of Tecumseh, eight kilometres west of Highway 27 and north of Highway 9.
**Open:** Year-round. Winter hours: 9:00 a.m. to 5:00 p.m. Summer hours: 9:00 a.m. to 8:00 or 9:00 p.m.
**Rates:** Hourly; two-hour and four-hour rides; special beginners' riding course; package prices available.
**Age Recommendations:** None. Children age five and up ride on their own mount. Younger children may ride double with a parent. Groups with small children go only at a walk or slow trot. Will divide the group and have the guide hold back the younger riders so the older and more experienced ones can do a slow canter or lope.
**Facilities and Services:** Trail rides. Offers trail rides of one hour, two hours, and four hours in length. The four-hour ride includes a lunch. The stable has thirty to forty Quarter Horses, Appaloosas, and part drafts. English and Western saddles. Helmets available.

Trail guides show beginners how to turn, stop, and start. The trail guide gives pointers along the trail.
**Terrain:** Open fields and some reforestation. The two- and four-hour rides include some road work. The four-hour ride goes back and forth to a nearby reforestation area.
**Other Services:**

- Day camps (see listing in Chapter 4).
- Riding lessons (see listing in Chapter 2).
- April and September courses for beginners organized through Bloordale Community School in Toronto. The program runs for seven weeks for two hours on Saturday mornings. It includes one hour of horse care and a one-hour lesson. Sign-up by individual session or for the whole course. For more information and sign-up, call Eileen Lee at (416) 394-8699.

- Experienced riders can get peppier horses if the guides feel confident they're able to control a better mount.

**Rocking Horse Ranch Stables**
11815 Yonge Street
R.R. #1
Richmond Hill, ON L4C 4X7
Phone: (905) 884-3292

$15.00 per hour (march break)
$20.00 per hour (weekends)
$18.00 per hour (regular rate)

should call for reservations.

**Location:** About five kilometres north of Major Mackenzie Drive or one kilometre south of Stouffville Road. Reach by GO transit from the Yonge and Finch station in Toronto. Take the Newmarket B bus. It will let you off at the gate.
**Open:** Year-round, 9:00 a.m. to dark. Closed Mondays, except holiday Mondays.
**Rates:** Hourly, higher on weekends and holidays.
**Age Recommendations:** Minimum age for trail rides is eight. Parents can lead younger children around a paddock area.
**Facilities and Services:** Supervised trail rides for the whole family. The stable has fifteen to twenty horses of Quarter Horse type. There is one large pony. Western saddles. No helmets.
**Terrain:** The trail ride goes through woods, hills, and open fields of a 300-acre farm.
**Other Services:**

- Lessons (see listing in Chapter 2).
- Hay rides booked in advance with a deposit.
- This stable will sometimes try to split the ride if the guide finds that some people are more capable than others.
- Experienced riders may get a lead horse if they have ridden there before and the owner has noticed that they can handle a mount.

Hours: 10:00-6:00
Rate!

**Windquest Trails**
16292 McCowan Road
R.R. #3
Newmarket, ON L3Y 4W1
Phone: (905) 473-3909

Hours: 10:00 4:00

Rate: $20.00

**Location:** West side of McCowan Road, three kilometres north of the Aurora Side Road. Fifteen minutes north of Toronto.
**Open:** Late April to mid-October, weather permitting. Dusk to dawn. By appointment only.
**Rates:** Hourly; higher on weekends; children up to age fourteen are at a lower rate than adults. Write for a brochure.
**Age Recommendations:** Eight and up, depending on the number and experience of people on the trail ride. Will take children between eight and ten out on the trail with other members of the same family. Will not take out rides with all young children.
**Facilities and Services:** Supervised trail rides through the Vivian Forest (York Regional Forest). Six trail horses, including Quarter Horses and Quarter Horse types. Western or English saddles. Helmets available and strongly recommended.

Beginners are mounted in a paddock where they are given a ten-minute lesson on how to make the horse turn, stop, and go. They are also assessed for their confidence. On the trail, the group moves as fast as the least confident rider.
**Terrain:** Wide sandy logging trails where riders often see deer, squirrels, and chipmunks. The occasional wolf and fox have been sighted.
**Other Services:**

- Riding lessons (see listing in Chapter 2).
- Horse and rider pick-up service for those who own their own horses.
- Birthday parties.
- Horse badges for Brownies and Guides.
- Pre-ride questions evaluate the ability of riders. There are a couple of more spirited horses for experienced riders.

## *East of Metro Toronto*

**Kuzenko Riding Stable**
R.R. #1
Hampton, ON L0B 1J0
Phone: (905) 725-5575

**Location:** On Courtice Road north of Highway 401 and east of Oshawa.
**Open:** Year-round, 11:00 a.m. to dusk. Reservations preferred.
**Rates:** Hourly.
**Age Recommendations:** None. It depends on whether the child's legs are long enough to reach the stirrups.
**Facilities and Services:** Trail riding. The stable has twenty-three mounts of various types. Western saddles. No helmets. Beginners receive a short introduction from the guide.
**Terrain:** Scenic trails through the bush and some open field.
**Other Services:**

- Experienced riders who are known by the guide can get a more challenging horse if they request one.

**Pleasure Valley**
2499 Brock Road
R.R. #4
Uxbridge, ON L9P 1R4
Phone: (905) 649-3334

**Location:** About three kilometres north of Claremont on the east side of Brock Road.
**Open:** April to November, depending on the weather.
**Rates:** Hourly; reduction for riding club members.
**Age Recommendations:** Minimum age is twelve. Younger children can be accommodated by phoning ahead and making special arrangements.
**Facilities and Services:** Horseback riding for teens and adults. The stable has thirty to thirty-six mounts ranging from pony to

draft size. Trail rides take twelve to fourteen riders on a guided tour. Western saddles. Helmets are optional.

Beginners receive a five-minute lesson to give them the basics of turning, stopping, and backing a horse.

**Terrain:** Trail rides criss-cross six hundred acres of meadows, woods, and pastures. From one section of trail, riders can see downtown Toronto, which is more than sixty kilometres away.

**Other Services:**

- Day camps (see listing in Chapter 4).
- Pleasure Valley is an entertainment park with waterslides, mini golf, picnic sites, roller-blading, swimming, and hay rides.
- Interested riders can join the riding club. Riding club members get reduced riding rates, can reserve specific horses, go out on their own, may take an approved guest riding, and have access to the park during the summer months.
- School excursions can be arranged in May/June and September/October. These include horse education, a trail ride, and the use of park facilities.

## *West of Metro Toronto*

### Five Star Ranch

3340 Dundas Street West
Oakville, ON L6J 4Z3
Phone: (905) 827-9578

**Location:** Dundas Street just west of Highway 25.

**Open:** Year-round, 10:00 a.m. to dusk. Seven days per week.

**Rates:** Hourly; less expensive with reservation; special rates for two-hour and four-hour rides.

**Age Recommendations:** None. Children age ten and under are allowed to walk and trot on the trail. Small children ride double with an adult at a walk. Adult rides include walk, jog or trot, and lope or canter.

**Facilities and Services:** Trail riding. The ranch has twenty-four trail horses of mixed type. Western saddles. Helmets are available.

Beginners are given a five-minute introduction in using the reins and making the horse move. The guide helps them along the trail.

**Terrain:** Good variety of trees, open fields, ravines, and rivers.

**Other Services:**

- Lessons (see listing in Chapter 2) and day camps (see listing in Chapter 4).
- Lessons for riders with disabilities. See Mobility Riders in Chapter 2.
- Five Star Ranch has horses at all levels. Trail guides try to gauge rider experience and assign a suitable horse. Experienced riders should outline their background.

**The Ranch**

5111 Highway 25
R.R. #1
Milton, ON L9T 2X5
Phone: (905) 876-4511

**Location:** On Highway 25 just south of Milton between the Queen Elizabeth Way and Highway 401.

**Open:** Year-round. Every day from 9:00 a.m. until dark.

**Rates:** Hourly.

**Age Recommendations:** Eight and up. Parents can rent a pony for younger children. The pony must be led around the paddock by the person accompanying the child.

**Facilities and Services:** Trail riding. The Ranch has twenty-five trail horses, including some ponies and smaller horses of the Quarter Horse and Appaloosa type. Most are quiet. Western saddles. Helmets are available.

Before riders get on a horse, the trail guides ask if they've ridden before. Guides offer instruction in how to get onto the horse, how to hold the reins, and how to turn. Along the trail, the guides are constantly watching riders and making suggestions about how to handle the different mounts.

**Terrain:** Scenic tours through various fields and forested areas. Some of the rides explore the area around Sixteen Mile Creek.

**Other Services:**

- Riding lessons (see listing in Chapter 2) and day camps (see listing in Chapter 4).
- Riders who take lessons automatically belong to The Ranch's Riding Club. Riding Club members who pass a riding competence test are allowed to choose the horse they want on the trail. Some can ride without supervision.
- Sleigh and hay rides.
- Moonlight rides.
- The Ranch will accommodate riders with physical or intellectual disabilities who are accompanied by family or staff willing to assist with safety measures.

**Rocky Ridge Ranch**
R.R. #2
Rockwood, ON N0B 2K0
Phone: (905) 854-2584

**Location:** North of Highway 401 between Highway 25 and Guelph Line.

**Open:** September to June by reservation only.

**Rates:** Hourly; family and groups rates.

**Age Recommendations:** Minimum age of nine on horses. Children under nine can ride a pony in the ring. If they show they are able to handle the pony, they can take it out on the trail.

**Facilities and Services:** Trail riding for children, teens, and adults. The stable has fifty-eight mounts ranging from large horses to approximately ten ponies. Western saddles. No helmets are available.

Every ride includes ten to fifteen minutes of instruction on how to mount and dismount, turn, and stop the horse. Riders practice for a few minutes in the ring before going out on the trail.

**Terrain:** Rolling and rugged hills of the Niagara Escarpment.

There are wooded sections as well as open trails.

**Other Services:**

- Overnight rides (see listing in Chapter 3) and residential summer camp (see listing in Chapter 4).
- Hay and sleigh rides by reservation. Minimum group size is ten.
- Overnight outings for schools and groups can be arranged. These require a minimum of ten people or a family group.

**Wildwood Manor Ranch**

R.R. #5
Georgetown, ON L7G 4S8
Phone: (905) 877-6852

**Location:** Northeast of Trafalgar Road and Highway 7.
**Open:** Year-round. By appointment only.
**Rates:** Hourly.
**Age Recommendations:** None. Small children can ride double with a guide or be led on a pony.
**Facilities and Services:** Trail riding. The Ranch has thirty-five trail horses. Western saddles. No helmets are available.

Beginners receive five to ten minutes of instruction in holding their reins, placing their feet properly in the stirrups, and asking the horse to stop, turn, and go.

**Terrain:** Fields and bush.

**Other Services:**

- Lessons (see listing in Chapter 2) and day camps (see listing in Chapter 4).
- Full sports facility including tennis courts, heated swimming pool, and large playing field.
- Picnic facilities.

Horseback camping can be enjoyed by the whole family.

Many riding stables offer hay rides for group outings.

As a safety precaution, many riding stables insist that all riders wear a well-fitting helmet with a chin strap.

Western saddles are designed to carry both a rider and pack gear.

English saddles are designed to give the rider close contact with the horse.

Trail riders using English saddles often carry their overnight gear in a backpack.

Barrel racing is a popular Western event.

A horse being longed moves in a circle around a handler on the ground. *Ontario Ministry of Agriculture and Food.*

Beginning riders should learn how to clean out a horse's feet with a hoof pick. *Ontario Ministry of Agriculture and Food.*

CHAPTER TWO

# Lesson Stables in the Metro Toronto Area

## STYLES OF RIDING

Although trail riding can be an enjoyable introduction to horseback riding, probably the best way to get the most out of your riding is to learn to handle a horse. Fortunately, there are a large number of lesson stables right in and around Metropolitan Toronto. Before signing up for lessons, however, you must decide on the style of riding you want to learn—English or Western.

### *English Riding*

English saddles are the small flat saddles you see on jumpers. Such saddles have several advantages. They're light. They allow the rider close contact with the horse, which makes it easier for people with good balance to give their mount directions. English saddles are also specially designed to allow the rider to take a horse over a jump safely.

Most English saddles have safety stirrups. If the rider's foot catches in the stirrup during a fall, the whole stirrup iron and leather will separate from the saddle without damaging either the saddle or the stirrup leathers.

Most riders begin by learning the basics: mounting and dismounting in safety, turning the horse, and asking it to go a number of gaits or speeds. English riders begin with flat work or work on the ground, as opposed to jumping. They learn to use their legs and back to make their mount walk, trot, and canter. They work to keep in balance at all gaits, and also learn to feel what is happening to the horse's body as it moves from a walk to a trot to a canter and back. As they become more comfortable, they learn to post. This is the term for raising and lowering the body in a controlled manner during the trot.

Once they have the basics, many English-style riders progress to other disciplines, including equitation, dressage, and jumping. Equitation is the art of horseback riding, focusing on the rider's correct riding position and use of the natural aids—hands, legs, seat, upper body, and mind. Dressage is the term for the careful schooling of horse and rider. Riders learn to control every movement of their mount, making them go forwards, backwards, and sideways at a variety of speeds. These are the horses that appear to dance under their riders.

Probably the most thrilling form of English riding is jumping. Before learning to do this properly, English riders often take forward seat lessons. These teach riders to move their weight forward to prepare for the changes in the horse's body and stride as it goes over a jump. If you've ever watched jumping classes on television, you've seen forward seat riding.

## *Western Riding*

Western saddles are the type that cowboys use. Many have high swells that help keep an unbalanced or novice rider in place. There's also a horn that was meant for roping cattle but doubles as a good hand-hold. Such saddles have several advantages for the beginner. First, many people feel more secure in them. The saddles are heavy and cover a large area of the horse's back. This distributes the weight of the rider over a comparatively large area and thus protects the horse's back from a jiggling and unbalanced beginner.

Unlike English saddles, Western saddles do not have safety stirrups. The stirrup is connected to the saddle with heavy leather straps that do not come off, even if the rider's foot gets caught during a fall. For this reason, it's especially important that riders wear cowboy boots or some other boot or shoe with a heel that will prevent their foot from slipping through the stirrup and possibly getting caught.

Western riders usually start by learning to pleasure ride. They learn to use their heels and weight to make their mount walk, jog (a slow trot), and lope (the Western term for a canter). They work to keep in balance with their horse at all of these speeds. Students may also learn to use their weight to move a horse from a walk to a trot to a canter and back.

Like many English riders, many Western riders don't go beyond the riding basics. Those that do often decide to specialize in certain types of events. Some take Western Equitation lessons to perfect their skills as a balanced rider. Those that like slow measured riding may take special lessons in pleasure or trail, two disciplines that emphasize the performance of the horse. Those that like speed and excitement may specialize in games that include racing around a series of barrels, bending around a row of poles, or performing other events at speed.

## THE STUDENTS

The beginner students of horseback riding can be divided into three general categories—children, adults, and people with disabilities. All can enjoy the benefits of taking riding lessons.

### *Children*

Although there are two- and three-year-olds who ride with skill and ease, these children usually have the advantage of at least one parent who rides. The family probably also owns a well-trained horse they trust with youngsters. For those without this advantage, it's best to wait until a child is between ten and twelve years old before starting lessons. At this age, children usually have the balance and coordination needed to learn to control a horse. Many also have confidence in their physical abilities, and are able to concentrate on the instruction.

It is possible to teach younger children how to ride, but the older ones learn faster and can usually advance from a walk to a trot within a couple of lessons.

### *Adults*

Don't let age stop you. Adults can and do learn to ride. In fact, I have friends who didn't ride a horse until they were in their fifties, and they became good riders. Depending on your physical abilities and dedication, you can become an extremely good rider—or simply learn enough to be able to enjoy peaceful country rides. The choice is yours.

The most difficult aspect of riding for beginner adults is learning to relax their body as they bump along on the back of a horse. Until they've learned to do that, anything above a walk can be jarring. But hundreds of adults learn this trick every year. If you're unsure of yourself, look for a stable that specializes in adult beginners.

Don't be discouraged if you don't find a compatible instructor the first time out. Many riding instructors have ridden since they were very young and don't understand what adults must come to terms with as they try to make their stiff bodies accommodate to the demands of the horse. Experienced riders who learned to ride in their late teens, or, even better, as adults, will often have the necessary patience and understanding to help other adults make that all-important step from complete beginner to confident novice.

### *Beginning Riders with Disabilities*

One of the great things about horseback riding is that it can be enjoyed by just about everybody, including people with intellectual, physical, or emotional disabilities. Information on facilities offering riding programs for children or adults with disabilities can be found in the following listings:

- Community Association for Riding for the Disabled (CARD) on page 33.
- The Therapeutic Riding Association for Challenged Kids (TRACK) on page 56.
- Mobility Riders on page 66.
- Foxhunter on page 43.
- The Riding Arts on page 49.
- Meadowlark Stables on page 65.
- Oxbow Ranch on page 88.
- Stewart Coughlin Riding Ranch on page 89.
- Lakeview Stables on page 86.
- Ostler Park Equestrian Centre on page 112.

## CHOOSING A LESSON STABLE

No matter what type of lessons you have decided to take, before choosing a stable, do a bit of shopping. Phone a couple of listings and discuss your needs with the stable contact. If you're an adult, ask how many adult beginners the stable has. Arrange to watch a lesson of these beginners. Watch their faces. Do they look relaxed and content? Or are they frustrated with the instructor's inability to explain equine terminology in understandable terms?

If you're looking for a placement for a child or teen, ask how many beginners of that age level the stable has, and arrange to watch one of the lessons. You may want to watch a series of lessons so that you can get some feel for how far your child might be able to progress at the particular stable.

Some stables start nonriders on a longe line. This is a long line the instructor uses to control the horse so that the rider only has to worry about balance. Lessons on a longe line are an excellent way for the beginning rider to learn how to balance on a moving horse. They are also useful for more advanced riders who wish to improve the way they sit on the horse and are often used by Olympic-level equestrians before major competitions.

### *Instructor Credentials*

Beginning riders who plan to ride solely for pleasure don't necessarily need to worry about whether or not their riding instructors have certified credentials—so long as the teacher is knowledgeable and competent.

If you're serious about showing, however, or want to make sure that you're doing everything correctly, look for a certified instructor. The Canadian Equestrian Federation has certification levels for both English and Western coaches. These instructors go through lessons in practical horse care and proper riding position that may give them an advantage over other instructors.

Another type of certification that many Ontario instructors have is through the British Horse Society, which offers coaching levels similar to those offered by the Canadian Equestrian Federation. Other instructors are not CEF certified, but have participated in Pony Club. Pony Club levels also provide an excellent grounding in safe ways to enjoy horses.

On the other hand, there are many excellent noncertified instructors. Many of these instructors have been involved with horses for a long period of time, have participated in many forms of riding, and want to share their knowledge of horses with others. Some of these instructors have many years of coaching experience and have just not taken the time to qualify for CEF certification.

Don't be surprised if you have difficulty finding a certified Western instructor. Because this certification is relatively new, there aren't that many Ontario riders who have taken the time to earn it. If you want to ride and show on the Western circuit, or are particular about the way you learn to sit a Western-trained horse, and can't find a CEF-certified coach, look for a stable involved in that kind of showing and request coaching from a sympathetic and experienced coach or rider. If you plan simply to ride for pleasure, look for an instructor who enjoys working with someone at your level.

## STABLE ETIQUETTE

Once you've chosen an instructor and made arrangements for your first lesson or group of lessons, check to find out what the stable expects from its students. Most stables expect riders to arrive twenty to thirty minutes before their lesson. This gives the riders time to groom and tack up their mount before the lesson begins. (Grooming is the term for brushing the horse and cleaning its feet. Tacking up refers to placing the proper saddle and bridle on the horse.) Riders are also expected to cool and untack their mounts after each lesson. Some stables also expect them to clean the tack.

If you're unable to take one of your lessons, call the stable as soon as possible. At some stables, you'll be expected to pay for the lesson anyway, since the horse and instructor have been reserved for you. Other stables will arrange make-up lessons. Either way, you should still call if you're sick or something unexpectedly delays your arrival.

## RIDING APPAREL

Dress appropriately. For indoor riding during the winter, this may mean wearing heavy sweaters that will keep you warm in the arena, and carrying a coat to put on after you've finished riding. For outdoor winter riding—which can be fun if you're prepared for it—dress for the worst. Wear thick boots with double socks, heavy gloves, and a windproof coat over heavy sweaters and long underwear.

Especially for adults, proper riding apparel can make the difference between a comfortable ride and one that leaves you with chafed legs and sore muscles. If you're going to take more than an occasional lesson, you may want to buy clothes that have been specifically designed for the type of lessons you're taking.

### *English Riding Apparel*

English riders can start with these basics:

- a helmet
- riding breeches, jodhpurs, or exercise pants
- riding or paddock boots
- riding gloves

There are several styles of riding helmets available today. The Pony Club helmet is a felt-covered hard hat with an inner lining of dense rubber foam that protects the rider's head in the event of a fall. The harness and chin strap are welded right to the helmet so that it won't come off during a fall.

Many stores also carry the new ASTM-approved helmets, which have been designed to dissipate a blow from something sharp. These helmets are tested in the United States and consist of a hard foam lining similar to that used in bicycle helmets. They protect the rider from a fall at high speed.

Like other safety equipment, riding helmets must fit properly. To check the fit, put on the helmet and adjust the chin strap. Move your head from side to side and up and down. If the helmet hurts, it's too small. If it slips forward or back, it's too big. You can make a large helmet smaller by fitting foam rubber into the interior lining, but it's better to purchase a helmet that fits properly.

Riding helmets should be replaced after a severe fall or if they are dropped from a height since this may reduce their protectiveness.

The advantage of proper riding pants is comfort. The seams on an ordinary pair of jeans run down the inside of the leg and the centre of the back. When you're horseback riding, those seams are going to rub your skin as you sit in the saddle or use your legs to signal your mount. Well-styled riding pants either have specially designed seams in these areas, or are designed so that the seams avoid parts of the anatomy that will come into contact with the horse or saddle.

Riding breeches are slightly shorter than regular pants. This allows them to slip into riding boots without bunching.

Jodhpurs have a loop that fits around the bottom of the

rider's foot. This prevents the pants from riding up, thus protecting the legs from chafing by the stirrup leathers. Although some jodhpurs will fit into regular riding boots, they are meant to be worn with paddock boots. Paddock boots look like leather shoes with ankle protection and a heel.

Exercise pants are the riding version of jogging pants. They are often less expensive than breeches or jodhpurs and are extremely comfortable.

### *Western Riding Apparel*

The basics of Western dressing are cowboy boots, pants, a Western shirt, and a cowboy hat. There is a wide range of Western wear that can be enjoyed around horses and do double duty as informal wear for a casual party or a square dance. In fact, you can buy riding boots to coordinate with just about any outfit you have. Look for a pair that don't pinch your toes. If you plan to use them for more than riding, you should walk around the store in them before buying—many aren't designed for walking.

Western-style riding pants are often made of a stretchy material that allows you to lift your leg high enough to mount with ease. To make sure they've got enough stretch, try doing a few deep knee bends. If they pull or bind at the knees or hips, look for a larger size.

Many riders like to buy a number of Western shirts that complement their pants, hat, hair, or favourite horse.

The traditional Western hat is a cowboy hat. However, with the modern emphasis on safety, hat/helmets have been designed. These are hats that look like a cowboy hat on the outside, but have the interior of a protective helmet.

## RIDING LESSON STABLE LISTINGS

### *Within Metro Toronto*

**Claireville Ranch**
P.O. Box 1082, Station C
Rexdale, ON M9V 2B3
Phone: (905) 794-0700

**Contact:** Barb Newland, or whoever answers the phone.
**Location:** Highway 7, approximately three kilometres west of Highway 427, on Claireville Conservation Road, which runs south of Highway 7. Take the Brampton bus along Highway 7.
**Type of Lessons:** Western. Basic CEF levels.
**Rates:** Buy four lessons at a time; special beginner package; must make up missed lessons within one month.
**Age Recommendations:** Ten and up.
**Student Requirements:** Riders must be dressed for comfort and safety. This includes wearing loose jeans, boots with a heel, and a close-fitting top.
**Facilities:** One outdoor ring. Games obstacles and a trail set-up.
**Instructor Qualifications:** CEF Level 1 and 2 coaches.
**Lesson Programs:** Private, semiprivate, and group lessons. Semiprivate lessons have two or three riders. Group maximum is ten riders. Group average is six to eight riders.
**Beginners' Programs:** A safe rider program is held on Saturday mornings. Riders sign up for one month of two-hour sessions: 8:00 a.m. to 10:00 a.m. Riders learn to lead, groom, tack, and mount a horse. They then learn to walk, stop, turn, and trot it. Most riders are able to ride on the trail by the fourth lesson. This beginners' session is the beginning of the CEF Level 1 program for riders.
**Other Services:**

- Riding stable (see listing in Chapter 1).
- CEF level testing.

**Community Association for Riding for the Disabled (CARD)**
4777 Dufferin Street
North York, ON  M3H 5T3
Phone: (416) 667-8600

**Contact:** Judy Wanless (volunteer coordinator) or Sandy Webster-Stolte (equestrian director).
**Location:** East side of Dufferin Avenue, two lights north of Finch, in G. Ross Lord Park. Take the TTC to the Wilson Station. Take the Wilson 105A bus north to the second light north of Finch. Walk in from there.
**Type of Lessons:** Riding lessons for people with intellectual or physical disabilities whose therapist or doctor has referred them for therapeutic horseback riding.
**Rates:** Charitable organization; lessons are free by arrangement.
**Student Requirements:** Correct riding shoes or boots with heel. Long pants. Comfortable clothing suited to weather. Recommends that students buy their own ASTM-approved helmet.
**Facilities:** Heated indoor arena with special accommodation for people with disabilities, including mounting ramps. Volunteers to assist with handling the horses and help the riders are always welcome. No horse experience necessary. CARD trains volunteers in the ways that are safe for disabled riders. The centre handles approximately 240 students between September and June, and another 110 in its summer program. There is a waiting list of about 300 riders. The stable has nineteen horses. Horses are rotated in and out of the program on a regular basis to give them time to relax. At any one time, three horses are usually out of the program relaxing in a pasture in the country, or working in smaller programs.
**Instructor Qualifications:** The equestrian director has a certificate from the North American Riding for Handicapped Association. Others have been certified by the Canadian Therapeutic Riders Association. Two-hour orientation sessions for the volunteers are held on Wednesdays from 7:20 p.m. to 9:20 p.m. They include instruction in how to use the special

ment in the centre, and an introduction to the CARD method of grooming, tacking, and leading. Safety is the main concern, and by making sure that all volunteers follow the same procedure, CARD offers a more secure environment for the CARD mounts.

**Lesson Programs:** Range from 1:1 with a therapist and three volunteers to group lessons (maximum of eight riders) in which individual riders have from one to three volunteers. There are two classes of independent riders who have a volunteer to assist with tacking and grooming.

**Beginners' Programs:** Beginner riders are assessed by an instructor and therapist. They are fitted for a helmet, and their height, weight, and medical record is checked. They are introduced to the instructors and volunteers who will work with them. Students and CARD representatives spend some time getting to know each other. After a tour of the barn and meeting the horses, new students are put on Peggy the Teaching Horse. This is a wooden horse covered with leather. Peggy's size and shape helps CARD staff determine a stirrup length adjustment for new riders. Peggy also has battery-operated indicators that light up when the rider uses proper turning aids. This helps instructors and therapists to assess whether the rider is capable of using proper rein aids. Information gathered during this introductory session is used to set therapeutic goals for the riding program.

**Other Services:**

- Volunteers may be able to become horse "mothers" and "fathers." These people offer special attention to CARD mounts, including grooming and training sessions. Prospective "mothers" and "fathers" must pass a riding and handling proficiency test.

**Exhibition Riding Club**
c/o 103 Miranda Avenue
Toronto, ON  M6B 4A2
Phone: (416) 393-6000

**Contact:** Ian Sloane, Stable Manager.
**Location:** Canadian National Exhibition Park. Take the Bathurst street car south from the Bathurst subway station into the CNE grounds. Walk across to the Horse Palace.
**Type of Lessons:** This stable covers all aspects of English riding, including riding on the flat and jumping.
**Rates:** By arrangement; riding club; introductory package.
**Age Recommendations:** Eight and up, depending on size.
**Student Requirements:** Helmet with a chin strap or harness. Boots with a heel. Any boot will do as long as it's narrow and has a flat sole with a low heel.
**Facilities:** Two indoor rings. Hunter and jumper courses are available. The stable has about eight school horses of the Quarter Horse type. They vary in size. Some will carry heavy adult riders.
**Instructor Qualifications:** British Horse Society and CEF certification.
**Lesson Programs:** Private and group. Groups of three to five. Because the stable runs as a riding club, students must take weekly lessons.
**Beginners' Programs:** Everyone starts with private lessons until the instructor feels confident that the novice rider can join a group. The stable offers an introductory package of three lessons, which provides the basics of grooming, tacking, and mounting. During these lessons, the instructor also assesses riding level.
**Other Services:**

- Some riding helmets for loan.
- Weekend clinics.
- Schooling shows for which students pay their own entry fee per class.
- Part-board on lesson horses for some riders.

**Humber College**
205 Humber College Drive
Etobicoke, ON M9W 5L7
Phone: (416) 675-5025

**Contact:** Equine Centre.
**Location:** Just south of Finch on the west side of Highway 27. Take the Wilson 96 bus from Wilson Station west to Humber College.
**Type of Lessons:** Courses include instruction from the beginning levels to CEF certification in Western and English coaching.
**Rates:** By the ten-week session; introductory courses are more expensive.
**Age Recommendations:** Eighteen and up.
**Student Requirements:** Solid boots or shoes with a low heel. Helmets are available at the Equine Centre.
**Facilities:** Large indoor and outdoor rings.
**Lesson Programs:** Offers ten-week sessions of riding three times a year: fall, winter, and spring. Group lessons with nine per class. Classes may have a waiting list, depending on demand.
**Beginners' Programs:** Prospective riders must attend an assessment night during which their skills are assessed. Beginning riders receive instruction in grooming and handling before they start to ride.
**Other Services:**

- Various theory courses also available.

**Rouge Hill Riding Centre**
1885 Rosefield Road
Pickering, ON L1Y 1A2
Phone: (416) 284-6176

**Contact:** Leanne Still or Shawn Thom.
**Location:** .5 kilometres east of Port Union Road on Highway 2. Take the Rouge Hill #13 bus from the Richmond Hill GO Station or at Meadowvale and Shepherd.
**Type of Lessons:** Offers Western equitation and pleasure

lessons. Teaches CEF Levels 1–4 in Western riding.
**Rates:** Forty-five-minute private lessons; one-hour semiprivate lessons; 1 1/2-hour group lessons; special winter rates from November to March.
**Age Recommendations:** Nine and up.
**Student Requirements:** Proper riding boots.
**Facilities:** Two outdoor rings. About twenty-two horses, including registered Quarter Horses, Appaloosas, Paints, and grade stock.
**Instructor Qualifications:** Two have CEF certified coaching levels. Other riders train students who are at least two CEF riding levels below them.
**Lesson Programs:** Adult lessons April to October, Monday to Thursday at 6:30 p.m. or 8:00 p.m. Children's (ages 9–16) lessons Saturdays only starting at 8:30 a.m. Group maximum is six riders; eight during the winter. Students must register at least one month in advance. November to March lessons are purchased as a package; the lessons are longer to give students a price break on winter riding. Package designed for riders aged 9–16.
**Beginners' Programs:** An introductory class for beginners is held in April.
**Other Services:**

- Riding stable (see listing in Chapter 1).
- After passing a proficiency test, students receive a Green Card, which allows them to take a trail ride without supervision.
- Monthly shows from April to October.
- CEF level testing.
- March Break Day Camp.

**Sunnybrook Stables**
P.O. Box 310, Station R
Toronto, ON  M4G 4C3
Phone: (416) 444-4044

**Contact:** Anita Barnes.
**Location:** Eglinton and Leslie in Sunnybrook Park. Take the

Eglinton bus east from Yonge Street to Leslie. It takes about fifteen minutes to walk through the park to the stable.
**Type of Lessons:** Offers English lessons, hunter, and dressage.
**Rates:** Different rates for private, semiprivate, and group lessons; lessons paid for in groups of four; special beginners' package of eight sessions.
**Age Recommendations:** Eight and up or thirty-two kilograms in weight.
**Student Requirements:** New type of ASTM-approved helmet. Boots or shoes with smooth soles and a small flat heel.
**Facilities:** Indoor arena. Two outdoor rings. Jumps available. The stable has twenty horses, including a mixture of registered and grade horses and a couple of ponies. Horses are rotated into the school on a regular basis to make sure that they're fresh.
**Instructor Qualifications:** CEF Level 1 coaching plus.
**Lesson Programs:** Lessons Monday to Thursday, 1:00 p.m. to 9:00 p.m.; Saturday and Sunday, 9:00 a.m. to 6:00 p.m. Closed Fridays. Private, semiprivate, and group. Group maximum is seven. Lessons are fifty minutes long. They are available in a series of four. No make-up lessons.
**Beginners' Programs:** Nonriders sign up for eight two-hour sessions from 6:00 p.m. to 8:00 p.m. on Tuesday evenings. Sessions include one hour in the barn and one hour in the arena. Up to sixteen beginners per session.
**Other Services:**

- Day camps (see listing in Chapter 4).
- Loaner helmets available.
- Six schooling shows per year: three in the spring, three in the fall.
- Pony Club sessions offered through this stable.
- Horse leasing and part-board program.

## *North of Metro Toronto*

**Aintree Farm**
R.R. #3
Newmarket, ON L3Y 4W1
Phone: (905) 836-6300

**Contact:** Tammy Galloway.
**Location:** East side of Warden Avenue, just south of Vivian Road.
**Type of Lessons:** Offers English dressage, jumper, and eventing lessons.
**Rates:** Private, semiprivate, and group lessons; thirty-minute private lessons; one-hour semiprivate and group sessions; prices by arrangement.
**Age Recommendations:** Sixteen and up.
**Student Requirements:** Most riders own or lease their own horses and already have their own equipment and riding apparel.
**Facilities:** Indoor arena. Outdoor Olympic-size dressage ring. Hunter and small cross-country course. Most mounts are private horses boarded at the facility. In order to help pay the bills, some boarders offer the use of their horses in return for payment of half the board. The number and type of available horses varies.
**Instructor Qualifications:** Nonresident instructors provide coaching in areas in which they are experts. Basic to advanced level.
**Lesson Programs:** Private, semiprivate, and group. Group maximum is three riders. Most students already know the riding basics.
**Other Services:**

- Show preparation for jumping, dressage, and three-day eventing.

**Coventry Manor**
R.R. #3, 18th Sideroad
King, ON L0G 1K0
Phone: (905) 841-1949 or (905) 841-3344

**Contact:** Jamie or Susie Smart.
**Location:** On St. John's Side Road (18th Sideroad) between Bathurst and Dufferin, about two minutes west of Aurora. The GO bus goes to Aurora from where the barn will pick up riders by arrangement.
**Type of Lessons:** Provides English lessons with a major focus on three-day eventing. Promotes ongoing learning and riding throughout the year. Handles beginner to advanced.
**Rates:** Private, semiprivate, and group lessons; lessons can be paid for individually or arranged in groups of four; practice rides; free introductory lesson.
**Age Recommendations:** Seven and up. The instructor feels that younger children do not get full value from lessons because their coordination and attention span are usually too limited.
**Student Requirements:** Riding breeches, boots, and helmet. Beginners can use jeans and shoes with a heel. After a month, they are encouraged to buy proper breeches.
**Facilities:** Indoor arena. Outdoor dressage and jumper rings. Cross-country course with two water jumps. Twelve school horses, including mounts at the beginner and intermediate level. Advanced riders can work on a retired Olympic mount.
**Instructor Qualifications:** Former Olympian who competed at the 1980 and 1988 Olympics, and in the 1987 and 1991 Pan American Games. Assisted by a CEF Level 1 coach.
**Lesson Programs:** Closed Mondays. Lessons on weekday evenings from 5:00 p.m. to 9:00 p.m., and all day Saturdays and Sundays. Some weekday afternoon private lessons. Private, semiprivate, and group lessons. Group maximum is four, usually groups have three riders. Students sign up for four lessons per month. There is one make-up lesson per month. Students may arrange practice rides between lessons.
**Beginners' Programs:** Introductory lessons are free. For experienced

riders new to the stable, this includes an assessment of riding ability so that they can be fit into the correct riding group. Nonriders are encouraged to take thirty-minute lessons on a longe line until they are familiar with the movement of the horse. These introductory longe lessons are at the same price as a group lesson. After one to two months, new riders are moved into a group.

**Other Services:**

- Coaches at shows and three-day events.
- Leases and part-boards horses to students.
- Three or four schooling shows per year.
- Clinics.

**Crossfield Farms Riding School**
9899 McCowan Road
R.R. #2
Markham, ON L3P 3J3
Phone: (905) 294-6934

**Contact:** Judy Brown.
**Location:** Southeast corner of McCowan and Major Mackenzie.
**Type of Lessons:** Offers English lessons. Novice to advanced. Flat work and jumping.
**Rates:** Private, semiprivate, and group; free introductory session.
**Age Recommendations:** Six and up.
**Student Requirements:** Helmet, boots, and a whip.
**Facilities:** Large indoor ring with viewing lounge. Four outdoor rings, including facilities for hunters, jumpers, and flat work. More than twenty-five school horses and ponies.
**Instructor Qualifications:** All have CEF Level 1 certification and are accomplished riders and teachers. Instructors are regularly evaluated by the barn manager.
**Lesson Programs:** Open Monday to Sunday, 9:00 a.m. to 9:00 p.m. Private, semiprivate, and group lessons. Group maximum is six riders. Students buy lessons in a series of four.
**Beginners' Programs:** Potential beginners are invited to a free

introductory session where they work 1:1 with an instructor during an hour-long session.

**Other Services:**

- New riders can borrow a helmet for the first couple of lessons.
- Riders are evaluated and move from level to level as their ability improves.
- Regular schooling shows and clinics.
- Practice rides monitored by an instructor.

**Earnscliffe Training Centre**
R.R. #1
Kettleby, ON L0G 1J0
Phone: (905) 841-1690

**Contact:** Martha Griggs or Susan Lang.
**Location:** Just north of Aurora Side Road, first street east of Highway 400.
**Type of Lessons:** Provides lessons to prepare horses and riders for three-day eventing.
**Rates:** Forty-five minute private lessons; one-hour semiprivate lessons.
**Age Recommendations:** Twelve and up.
**Student Requirements:** Helmet. Proper boots with a heel, NOT laced workboots. Breeches. Gloves.
**Facilities:** Indoor arena. Outdoor sand ring and dressage ring. Cross-country course and jumper course. Good hacking. Two lesson horses. Thoroughbreds that are former competitive mounts.
**Instructor Qualifications:** CEF Level 2 coach. Martha Griggs represented Canada at the 1984 Olympics. She is involved in the elite rider and CEF coaching programs, and is president of the Ontario Horse Trials Association.
**Lesson Programs:** Closed Mondays. Open 8:30 a.m. to 9:30 p.m. Tuesday to Sunday. Mainly private and semiprivate lessons. Some clinics during the nonshowing season.

**Beginners' Programs:** Most riders already know the basics.
**Other Services:**

- Full competitive package including transportation to show and show-day coaching.
- Working student program that trains students through summers and holidays.
- March break resident or day camp.
- Full- and half-day clinics provided on and off the property.
- Horses trained.

**Foxhunter**
4341 Stouffville Rd.
R.R. #4
Stouffville, ON L4A 7X5
Phone: (905) 640-5544

**Contact:** Alan Plewis.
**Location:** South side of Stouffville Road, .5 kilometres west of McCowan and six kilometres east of Highway 404.
**Type of Lessons:** Provides English lessons with emphasis on hunter/jumper and equitation.
**Rates:** Private, semiprivate, and group lessons; private lessons arranged on an individual basis; semiprivate and group lessons organized by the month; practice sessions; introductory lessons.
**Age Recommendations:** Nine and up. Children younger than that can ride with a caution to parents that the child may not be mentally or physically ready. Alan Plewis encourages parents to start young children during the warm summer months because winter riding can be very difficult for them.
**Student Requirements:** Boots that come above the ankle, have a heel designed not to hook in the stirrup, and a smooth sole. Prefer proper riding boots. Helmet with a harness. Adults may sign a waiver and go without the helmet. Stretch pants that do not wrinkle at the knee, are not slippery, and allow the rider to mount and take the proper riding position.
**Facilities:** Indoor arena. Outdoor jumper and hunter ring.

Cross-country course with two water jumps. Seventeen school horses, including Quarter Horse/Thoroughbred crosses and five ponies. The mixture of sizes allows for young children to heavy adult riders.

**Instructor Qualifications:** CEF Level 1 coach who is working on Level 2 certification. Uncertified instructors with a lot of experience and good teaching skills.

**Lesson Programs:** Private, semiprivate, and group lessons. Group maximum is six. Riders save money by signing up on a monthly basis. Unsupervised practice sessions can be arranged. About 20 per cent of the clientele are beginners. The farm can give them instruction and coaching so that they are capable of showing on the Trillium and A Circuits.

**Beginners' Programs:** Private and semiprivate introductory lessons introduce the novice to grooming, tacking, and riding. Riders new to the stable are assessed at this time. Complete beginners are encouraged to take several private lessons before they join a group at their level.

**Other Services:**

- Can rent or buy riding boots and helmets on the premises.
- Schooling shows from April to October.
- Coaching at Trillium Shows.
- Will take riders with disabilities on an individual basis.
- Large tack shop with new and second-hand equipment.
- Half-board on a lesson horse or share the board with an interested owner.

**Harrogate Hills Riding School**
Box 106
Gormley, ON L0H 1G0
Phone: (905) 887-5595

**Contact:** Patricia Gillis.

**Location:** On the Stouffville Sideroad, one kilometre west of Highway 404.

**Type of Lessons:** Offers English lessons.

**Rates:** Private, semiprivate, and group lessons; hour-
break on semiprivate and group sessions.
**Age Recommendations:** Seven and up. The oldest rid
married couple in their mid-seventies.
**Student Requirements:** Boots or shoes with a half-in heel.
Loose track pants. Helmets.
**Facilities:** Indoor arena and outdoor sand ring. One hundred acres of hacking. Jumps available. Approximately nineteen school horses, including Thoroughbreds and Thoroughbred-type.
**Instructor Qualifications:** CEF Level 1 or British Horse Society certification. Noncertified instructors have a lot of experience.
**Lesson Programs:** Tuesday to Sunday, all day and evenings. Private, semiprivate, and group lessons. Group maximum is six riders. Students sign up for two-month sessions. No make-up lessons.
**Beginners' Programs:** Beginners start in groups of two to six riders. They work with an instructor who has several riding assistants, usually one per beginner.
**Other Services:**

- Day camps (see listing in Chapter 4).
- Riding helmets loaned to beginners.
- Schooling shows every month from May to August.

**Leitchcroft**
463 Highway 7 East
Thornhill, ON  L3T 4B8
Phone: (905) 889-1730

**Contact:** Farm Office.
**Location:** On south side of Highway 7 just east of Bayview. Available by Markham transit or TTC's Don Mills bus, which goes via Leslie Street.
**Type of Lessons:** English—basic flat work, eventing, and dressage.
**Rates:** Group lessons only; pay by the month; special beginner package; free assessment lesson.
**Age Recommendations:** Ten and up.
**Student Requirements:** Hard hat with chin strap. Proper riding boots.

**Facilities:** Three indoor arenas. Three outdoor rings. Cross-country training course. Hunter and jumper fences available. About thirty school horses, including Quarter Horses and Quarter Horse types for beginners, and Thoroughbreds and Thoroughbred types for the more advanced.
**Instructor Qualifications:** Includes CEF and British Horse Society certification. One instructor has coached the Three-Day Event team.
**Lesson Programs:** Lessons on week nights and Saturday mornings. Group only. Hour-long. Maximum of six per group. Sign up by the month. Receive four or five lessons depending on the month.
**Beginners' Programs:** Summer courses for nonriders include two-week sessions of two hours per day, five days a week. Riders new to the school receive a fifteen-minute assessment to evaluate their skills before they are put into a class at their age and ability level.
**Other Services:**

- One schooling show per month.
- Coaches on eventing and dressage circuit.

**Maple Hill Farm**
R.R. #3
King City, ON L0G 1K0
Phone: (905) 727-5632

**Contact:** Jane Cocks, Linda Hauck, or Christi Pabst.
**Location:** On Dufferin just south of Aurora Side Road. Take the GO bus to Bloomington Side Road. Walk north.
**Type of Lessons:** English lessons. Hunter/jumper and three-day eventing.
**Rates:** Private, semiprivate, and group lessons; lower rate for semiprivate and group lessons; practice sessions at variable rates.
**Age Recommendations:** Most students are between the ages of twelve and fifty. There are a lot of first-time adults.
**Student Requirements:** Hard hat and proper footwear.

**Facilities:** Indoor arena. Outdoor dressage and hunter/jumper rings. About six school horses, including a variety of safe and sensible mounts. Heated viewing lounge. Cross-country course.
**Instructor Qualifications:** Includes instructors with many years experience riding, training, and competing at advanced levels. One instructor has her Pony Club Level A and has ridden advanced level three-day eventing. Another has been showing on the recognized circuit for fifteen years and is provincial champion in the jumper division.
**Lesson Programs:** Lessons at varied times by arrangement. Private, semiprivate, and group. Hour-long. Three to five riders per group. Practice sessions available.
**Beginners' Programs:** Nonriders start in short private lessons until they are ready to join a group. Usually this is after three or four lessons. New riders take a private assessment lesson to determine their level before joining a group.
**Other Services:**

- Loans helmets for the first couple of lessons.
- Series of winter clinics in jumping, dressage, and hunter/jumper.
- Monthly schooling shows from April to October.

**Pinedale Quarter Horses**
15443 Ninth Line
R.R. #3
Stouffville, ON L4A 7X4
Phone: (905) 640-1587

**Contact:** Dianne Howe.
**Location:** Two kilometres east of Highway 48 on the Ninth Line, .5 kilometres north of Aurora Side Road.
**Type of Lessons:** This is a breeding, training, and show stable that provides lessons for potential horse owners. English and Western.
**Rates:** Private and group at the same rate; hour-long lessons.
**Age Recommendations:** Five and up. The stable has taught students up to seventy years old. It currently has several fifty-

year-old students who ride to release the stress caused by their busy careers.
**Student Requirements:** Hard hat. Gloves. Good boots with a heel.
**Facilities:** Indoor arena. Outdoor lighted pen. Access to Vivian Forest for trail riding. School horses include Quarter Horses used on the show circuit.
**Instructor Qualifications:** Twenty years in the horse business as a rider, teacher, and trainer. Students have won numerous American Quarter Horse Association and provincial year-end awards.
**Lesson Programs:** By appointment only. Maximum of two in a group. Two groups may work together to simulate a show situation. Lessons bought as a package of ten. Lessons are geared to showing. English lessons include training in equitation, hunter under saddle, hunter over fences, and driving. Western lessons include training in equitation, horsemanship, trail, pleasure, halter, and showmanship.
**Beginners' Programs:** Suggest one lesson before deciding on a package. Introduction geared to safety around horses and horsemanship.
**Other Services:**

- Six schooling shows per year.
- Part-boards and leases horses.

**Redstone Farm**
R.R. #1
Richmond Hill, ON L4C 4X7
Phone: (905) 884-2555

**Contact:** Stable Manager.
**Location:** On Elgin Mills East, just north of Major MacKenzie Drive between Bayview and Highway 404. Ten-minute walk from the Richmond Hill via Bayview bus stop.
**Type of Lessons:** English.
**Rates:** Private and semiprivate are the same rate; special rate for group lessons; practice sessions. Instead of offering make-up lessons,

this stable transfers the credit to the next month's lesson cost.
**Age Recommendations:** Eight and up.
**Student Requirements:** Boots with a heel. Helmet with welded harness.
**Facilities:** Indoor arena. Outdoor ring. Cross-country course. Other jumps. About twelve horses of mixed breed handling from beginning to advanced riders.
**Instructor Qualifications:** Some have CEF certification. The beginners' instructors are more advanced riders in the barn.
**Lesson Programs:** Monday to Thursday to 10:00 p.m., Friday to 8:00 p.m., Saturday and Sunday to 6:00 p.m. Private, semiprivate, and group. Group maximum is nine riders. Most groups have five or six students. Register on a monthly basis.
**Beginners' Programs:** Start with a group of beginners.
**Other Services:**

- Day camps (see listing in Chapter 4).
- Rents helmets.
- Part-boards school horses.
- Three or four schooling shows per year.

**The Riding Arts**
11181 Woodbine Avenue
Markham, ON L6C 1J4
Phone: (905) 887-9908

**Contact:** Gail Livitsanis.
**Location:** North side of Elgin Mills, west of Woodbine.
**Type of Lessons:** Offers English and Western lessons. Specializes in English dressage and jumping, plus Western performance. The instructor trains riders to show specifications on her competitive level horses.
**Rates:** Private, semiprivate, and group lessons; hour-long sessions; thirty-minute assessment lesson.
**Age Recommendations:** Nine and up. One student started riding at sixty-seven years of age and now, at seventy-three, is showing in dressage.

**Student Requirements:** Helmets are available for beginners. Students are advised not to buy equipment until they are sure about their riding plans. When they've made a decision, the instructor will help them decide what equipment they need and what fits their budget.
**Facilities:** Indoor and outdoor rings plus hacking facilities. Jumping and cross-country courses, a trail set-up, and dressage ring. Can set up for Western games and performance.
**Instructor Qualifications:** British Horse Society level from an Instructor's Course given by a fellow of the British Horse Society.
**Lesson Programs:** Group maximum is four riders at the same level. Students start with private lessons, move to semiprivate when they're able to cope with the horse and its movements, then can move to a group lesson if they fit in with the group. Students usually sign up for a course of four lessons, depending on their needs and budget.
**Beginners' Programs:** New riders start with a half-hour assessment lesson on the longe. The instructor observes their balance, coordination, and ability to cope with the horse and its movement. From there, students are fit into the school.
**Other Services:**

- Helmets available for beginners.
- The instructor is a former CARD instructor who has worked with riders with physical and intellectual disabilities as well as with disadvantaged kids.

**Rocking Horse Ranch Stables**
11815 Yonge Street
R.R. #1
Richmond Hill, ON L4C 4X7
Phone: (905) 884-3292

**Contact:** Joan Staff.
**Location:** About five kilometres north of Major Mackenzie Drive or one kilometre south of Stouffville Road. Take GO transit from the Yonge and Finch station. Take the Newmarket B

bus. It will let you off at the gate.
**Type of Lessons:** Offers Western-style lessons for the beginner.
**Rates:** Private and semiprivate; hourly lessons.
**Age Recommendations:** Ten and up. The owner believes that younger children do not have the strength, coordination, or size to control horses on the trail.
**Facilities:** The stable has fifteen to twenty horses of Quarter Horse type. There is one large pony.
**Instructor Qualifications:** Forty years riding experience, showing experience, and has run a trail riding stable for eleven years.
**Lesson Programs:** Private and semiprivate. Goal of the lessons is to get riders comfortable on a pleasure horse so that they can enjoy trail riding and possibly move to their own horse. The lessons are outdoors, and most of them include a trail ride.

**Windquest Trails**
16292 McCowan Road
R.R. #3
Newmarket, ON L3Y 4W1
Phone: (905) 473-3909

**Contact:** John or Cathy Alden.
**Location:** West side of McCowan Road, three kilometres north of Aurora Side Road. Fifteen minutes north of Toronto.
**Type of Lessons:** Offers Western and English lessons. Specializes in Western pleasure and speed events.
**Rates:** Group lessons; 1 1/2 hours.
**Age Recommendations:** Eight and up. Will handle younger children on an individual basis.
**Student Requirements:** Boots or shoes with a half-inch heel. Helmets.
**Facilities:** Outdoor sand ring and trails. Six school horses, including Quarter Horses and Quarter Horse types.
**Instructor Qualifications:** CEF Level 1 coaches (minimum). Many years experience riding and showing in Western events, including being former Ontario Barrel Racing Association Champion.

**Lesson Programs:** Thursday, Friday, and Saturday mornings during the summer months. Lessons are 1 1/2 hours long: thirty minutes of grooming and horse-safety instruction, thirty minutes of riding instruction, and thirty minutes of trail riding on wide sandy forest trails. Group lessons for beginners. Maximum of five in group. Private and semiprivate by arrangement.
**Beginners' Programs:** Two certified adult coaches usually available for beginner lessons. One will concentrate on the beginning rider and spend extra time on the riding introduction. The emphasis is on safely having fun around horses.
**Other Services:**

- Trail riding (see listing in Chapter 1).

## *East of Metro Toronto*

### Fieldstone Farm

R.R. #2
Uxbridge, ON L9P 1R2
Phone: (905) 852-6372

**Contact:** Penny McEachern.
**Location:** Twenty minutes east of Highway 404 and north of Davis Drive.
**Type of Lessons:** English lessons specializing in hunter/jumper and equitation. Handles beginner to advanced.
**Rates:** Private and group lessons; hour-long.
**Age Recommendations:** Six and up.
**Student Requirements:** Hard hat. Work boots or children's rain or winter boots that cover the ankle and have a heel.
**Facilities:** Indoor arena. Three outdoor rings, including two hunter and one jumper course. Two horses and five ponies, including retired show animals of good quality.
**Instructor Qualifications:** British Horse Society certification and twenty-one years of experience teaching other riders. Trained four 1992 provincial champions in hunter/jumper and equitation.

**Lesson Programs:** Lessons after school Tuesday to Friday; Saturday and Sunday all day. Closed Mondays. Private and group. Group maximum is five riders. There are usually only three or four per lesson.
**Beginners' Programs:** During the summer, there are six-week packages for nonriders. Or, nonriders can start in private lessons until they're able to post. They then join a group for beginners. Riders new to the stable take a private assessment lesson before joining a group at their riding level.
**Other Services:**

- Day camps (see listing in Chapter 4).
- Loaner helmets.
- Part-boards and leases horses to lesson students.
- One in-house and one open schooling show per year.
- Coaches on the Trillium Show circuit.
- Hosts a Trillium Show in July.
- Trailering.
- Boarding facility with excellent hacking, oversized indoor arena, and three sand outdoor rings.

**The Pickering Horse Centre**
3900 Paddock Road
R.R. #2
Claremont, ON L1V 2P9
Phone: (905) 649-1342

**Contact:** Gary Yaghdjian or Clare Elcock.
**Location:** East along Highway 7 from Brock Road.
**Type of Lessons:** Offers English lessons with emphasis on hunter/jumper.
**Rates:** Private, semiprivate, and group lessons; thirty-minute or one-hour private lessons; one-hour semiprivate and group lessons.
**Age Recommendations:** Nine and up.
**Student Requirements:** Helmet. Boots that cover the ankle and have a low heel. Long pants.
**Facilities:** Indoor arena. Three outdoor areas. Hunter and

jumper courses. About sixteen horses of a variety of types and sizes from beginner to competitive level.
**Instructor Qualifications:** CEF certified or in the process.
**Lesson Programs:** Open daily. Lessons by arrangement. Private, semiprivate, and group. Group maximum is six riders. Students sign up by the month. Make-up lessons if the barn cancels.
**Other Services:**

- Active on Trillium Circuit.
- Home of Rouge Valley Pony Club.
- Hosts Pony Club, Trillium, and Schooling shows.
- Hunter/jumper clinics.
- Leases horses.

**Southbreeze**
R.R. #1
Locust Hill, ON L0H 1J0
Phone: (905) 472-8224

**Contact:** Christine or Brian Murphy.
**Location:** Five kilometres west of Brock Road on Highway 7.
**Type of Lessons:** English and Western riding lessons. This is a noncompetitive barn with a casual atmosphere.
**Rates:** Private, semiprivate, and group lessons; hour long; reasonable rates. First lesson for nonriders is private but charged at the group rate.
**Age Recommendations:** Seven and up. The owners feel that most children younger than this are really only getting a supervised pony ride.
**Student Requirements:** Boots with a heel. All juniors wear a helmet with a welded chin harness. Adults over twenty-five years old may ride without a helmet on the flat, but must wear one when jumping.
**Facilities:** Indoor arena. Large outdoor ring. Three round pens. Access to long trails. Approximately ten to twelve horses and ponies, predominantly Quarter Horses, Paints, Appaloosas, and Pintos.
**Instructor Qualifications:** The Western instructor is working

on her CEF Level 1 Western certification. The English instructor has years of show and lesson experience.

**Lesson Programs:** By appointment or drop by to see facility. Private, semiprivate, and group. Group maximum is six riders. Beginners ride in a group of three. Students sign up by the month. Make-up lessons can be arranged. Informal practice sessions arranged on a work-for-ride basis.

**Beginners' Programs:** During first private lesson, beginners are shown how to groom and tack before mounting. Beginners are then put in a small group of no more than three riders. There are usually one or more ground assistants.

**Other Services:**

- Adventure rides (see listing in Chapter 3).
- Part-boards horses.
- Ground sessions.
- Trailers to local shows.

**Tanglewood**

164 Cemetery Road
R.R. #1
Uxbridge, ON L9P 1R1
Phone: (905) 852-7180

**Contact:** Kathi Leeson.

**Location:** Southwest corner of Highway 47 and Cemetery Road, just south of Uxbridge, close to the town limits. Take the GO Bus from the Scarborough Town Centre to Uxbridge. It stops at the corner.

**Type of Lessons:** Offers English riding lessons with emphasis on hunter/jumper.

**Rates:** Private, semiprivate, and group lessons; hour-long; semiprivate and group at lower rates; practice sessions; evaluation lessons.

**Age Recommendations:** Seven and up. Younger riders may be accepted after an individual evaluation. Some highly motivated children have the physical and mental capability to learn to ride at a younger age. Some do not.

**Student Requirements:** Suggests gloves and boots with a heel. Encourages riders to make do with equipment they already own until they decide whether or not they will ride for a period of time. Many children ride in track pants or schooling sweats.
**Facilities:** Indoor arena. Outdoor hunter ring. About fifteen school horses, including ponies and large horses from beginner to advanced level. Some Thoroughbreds and Warmbloods.
**Instructor Qualifications:** Working on CEF Level 2 coaching certification.
**Lesson Programs:** Open daily, 9:00 a.m. to 10:00 p.m. Group maximum is six riders. Students sign up by the calendar month.
**Beginners' Programs:** Nonriders receive a 1 3/4-hour introductory lesson during which they learn about grooming and tacking, then ride for one hour. Depending on their ability, they are fit into a group, or encouraged to continue with private or semiprivate lessons until they have the ability to ride with a larger group. Other riders are assessed during a one-hour evaluation lesson before being fit into the school.
**Other Services:**

- Day camps (see listing in Chapter 4).
- Loans helmets to beginners.
- Leases competition horses.
- Coaches to show on Trillium Circuit.

**Therapeutic Riding Association for Challenged Kids (TRACK)**
R.R. #1
Uxbridge, ON L9P 1R1
Phone: (905) 852-6591

**Contact:** Sandi Vasey or Dee Cuthbertson.
**Location:** South of Davis Drive, just west of Uxbridge.
**Type of Lessons:** TRACK uses volunteers to assist in a riding program for children with physical disabilities. It takes rider referrals from physiotherapists and by assessment.
**Rates:** Variable price depending on the amount of fund-raising;

this is a charitable organization.
**Student Requirements:** Changes according to the rider's needs and disability.
**Facilities:** Indoor arena. Outdoor ring.
**Lesson Programs:** Riding program by arrangement only. Size of group and number of volunteers varies according to ability. The maximum amount of assistance is one leader and two side-walkers per horse. The minimum is one leader per horse.
**Beginners' Programs:** TRACK runs introductory programs for volunteers interested in becoming leaders and side-walkers. Beginning riders receive an assessment lesson. A physiotherapist is usually in attendance.

**Velvet Lane**
R.R. #3
Mount Albert, ON L0G 1M0
Phone: (905) 473-2039

**Contact:** Chris or Jim Young.
**Location:** Two farms north of Davis Drive on the 2nd Concession of Uxbridge, west of Uxbridge.
**Rates:** Private only; reasonable rates.
**Type of Lessons:** English lessons specializing in dressage and hunter.
**Age Recommendations:** Eight and up.
**Student Requirements:** Hard hat. Boots with a heel. Breeches or stretch pants. Gloves recommended. The instructor encourages riders to buy what they can afford and upgrade as they get more involved.
**Facilities:** Two outdoor rings, including a sand ring and one with jumps. One Quarter Horse lesson horse that is trained to medium level dressage and can jump 3'6".
**Instructor Qualifications:** CEF Level 1 coach.
**Lesson Programs:** Lessons any time by arrangement. Private only.
**Other Services:**

- Freelance coaching off the farm.

- Coaches at shows.
- Lesson students can arrange to use the school horse at shows.
- Horse transport.
- Breaking and training of young horses.

## *West of Metro Toronto*

**Blue Haven Farm**
R.R. #2
Brampton, ON L6V 1A1
Phone: (905) 843-3305

**Contact:** Linda Hoodem.
**Location:** West of Highway 10 and north of Highway 7 bypass, 1.5 kilometres north of the Mayfield and Chingacousy intersection on the left-hand side of Chingacousy.
**Type of Lessons:** English riding lessons. Specializes in hunter/jumper and showing. Takes riders through a series of levels, including beginner, novice, novice/intermediate, and intermediate.
**Rates:** Private and group lessons; one hour; private by special arrangement; lessons organized in groups of ten sessions; practice sessions; introductory package; nonriding clinics.
**Age Recommendations:** Six and up. Because most six-year-olds have a limited attention span for organized instruction, the stable prefers to start eight-year-olds.
**Student Requirements:** Boots with a heel, preferably soft rubber or leather boots. No cowboy boots allowed. A properly fitted helmet with a chin strap. Suggests chaps or breeches.
**Facilities:** Indoor arena. Outdoor sand ring. Wash stalls. Hunter course set-up. This stable has approximately twelve school horses of mixed breeds, including Thoroughbreds, Thoroughbred/Arab crosses, and Quarter Horses. Emphasis is on mounts of athletic ability that can jump easily.
**Instructor Qualifications:** One is working on CEF Level 1

coaching certification, and others have coaching and showing experience. There is a qualified CEF Level 3 coach for advanced riders.

**Lesson Programs:** Lessons offered Monday to Thursday evening, and all day Saturday. Some daytime lessons. Private and group. Group maximum is six when working inside and eight in the outdoor rings. Riders sign up for ten lessons at a time. If they miss a lesson, it will be tacked on to the end of their series. The top stable riders show on the Trillium Circuit. Practice sessions are on Sundays and Fridays during the day.

**Beginners' Programs:** The first beginner lesson is private and is divided between horse care and practical horse management. Riders new to the stable are put into a beginner group, assessed, and moved into the group where they belong.

**Other Services:**

- Practical sessions in tail and mane braiding, tack selection and care, bandaging, mane-pulling, etc.
- Schooling shows on first Sunday of March, April, May, October, November, and December.
- Clinics.
- Coaches on Trillium Circuit.
- Attends local schooling and pony shows.
- Leases and part-boards horses.

**Brain Manor Farm**
R.R. #1
Norval, ON L0P 1K0
Phone: (905) 877-1257

**Contact:** Victoria McDonald.

**Location:** Northeast of Trafalgar Road and Highway 401, northwest of Winston Churchill and Highway 401.

**Type of Lessons:** English riding lessons. Specializes in hunter/jumper. Also has some boarded private horses which can be used for lesson purposes.

**Rates:** Private lessons only; by arrangement.

**Age Recommendations:** Ten and up. Riders must be tall

enough that their legs can give the aids when they're mounted.
**Facilities:** Indoor arena. Outdoor sand ring. Wooded trails. Jumps. This stable usually has about two lesson horses of Thoroughbred type.
**Instructor Qualifications:** Ridden on the hunter/jumper circuit, continues to take training.
**Lesson Programs:** Private only.
**Other Services:**

- Will take students to shows if they have their own horse.

**Creditview Stables**
R.R. #10
Brampton, ON L6V 3N2
Phone: (905) 451-8654

**Contact:** Jim Rush.
**Location:** Creditview Road between Steeles and Derry Road.
**Type of Lessons:** English lessons. Specializes in hunter/jumper.
**Rates:** Private and group lessons; one hour; group sign-up by the month.
**Age Recommendations:** Nine and up.
**Student Requirements:** Helmet and boots with a heel.
**Facilities:** Indoor arena. Outdoor arena. Jumps are available. Approximately fifteen lesson horses, including large pony to horse size.
**Instructor Qualifications:** British Horse Society certification.
**Lesson Programs:** Lessons 4:30 p.m. to 9:30 p.m., Tuesday to Saturday. Sunday and Monday off. Private and group lessons. Maximum of seven riders per group. Make-up lessons are available.
**Beginners' Programs:** New riders fill out a form outlining their experience and what days they are available for lessons. Riders new to the stable are assessed in a group lesson at their estimated level. Nonriders start in a beginner class with at least one ground assistant helping the instructor.
**Other Services:**

- Day camps (see listing in Chapter 4).

- Loans helmets.
- Two schooling shows per year.

**Five Star Ranch**
3340 Dundas Street West
Oakville, ON L6J 4Z3
Phone: (905) 827-9578

**Contact:** Gail Haynes.
**Location:** Dundas Street just west of Highway 25.
**Type of Lessons:** Basic Western riding lessons.
**Rates:** Group lessons; 1 1/2 hours long; sign-up by group of ten lessons; special children's programs of eight thirty-minute lessons.
**Age Recommendations:** Eleven and up.
**Facilities:** Indoor arena. Outdoor arena. Some games equipment and trail obstacles. Approximately twenty-four horses.
**Instructor Qualifications:** CEF coaching certification in Western.
**Lesson Programs:** Lessons 10:00 a.m. to 10:00 p.m. Private and semiprivate by arrangement. Concentrates on group lessons. Sells a series of ten 1 1/2-hour group lessons. Group maximum is ten. Special program for children between the ages of five and ten. They sign up for ten thirty-minute lessons that concentrate on helping them learn balance, coordination, and control. Maximum of eight per group. Parents are encouraged to participate in the lessons by assisting from the ground.
**Beginners' Programs:** Beginners are given safety instructions on working around the horse. They learn to lead a horse in and out of its stall, and how to groom and tack. During basic riding instruction, they work with other beginners in a group. Riders new to the school receive an assessment lesson by arrangement.
**Other Services:**

- Trail rides (see listing in Chapter 1) and day camps (see listing in Chapter 4).
- Practical horse care sessions.

- Sessions to introduce riders to the show ring focusing on showmanship, horsemanship, pleasure, and barrel racing.
- An introduction to trail riding teaches riders how to deal with obstacles such as a bridge and gate.
- Also see the listing for Mobility Riders in this chapter.
- Write for a free pamphlet outlining other offerings.

**Halton School of Equitation**
1470 Steeles Avenue
R.R. #2
Hornby, ON L0P 1E0
Phone: (905) 826-2889

**Contact:** Auriel Halliday or Mary Courtney.
**Location:** South side of Steeles, 1.5 kilometres east of Trafalgar Road.
**Type of Lessons:** English riding lessons. Specializes in hunter/jumper.
**Rates:** Private, semiprivate, and group lessons; thirty-minute private and semiprivate lessons; one-hour group lessons; group sign-up by series of four or twelve lessons.
**Age Recommendations:** Eight and up.
**Student Requirements:** Hard hat with harness. Boots with a heel.
**Facilities:** Two indoor arenas. Three outside rings. One lighted sand ring. Permanent hunter course. Jumper course in summer. Approximately thirty school horses of various breed and breed types, as well as five ponies.
**Instructor Qualifications:** Most have CEF Level 1 coaching certification. Some have CEF Level 2 or British Horse Society coaching certification.
**Lesson Programs:** Lessons offered Monday to Thursday, Saturday and Sunday. Fridays off. This stable takes riders at the beginner to advanced levels. It works riders through different levels: three at the beginner stage, two at intermediate, and one for advanced. Private, semiprivate, and group lessons. Group maximum is five in the small arena, eight in the large arena.

**Beginners' Programs:** Nonriders are put together with others of similar age. They learn the ground basics before getting on the horse.
**Other Services:**

- Day camps (see listing in Chapter 4).
- Schooling shows.
- Trillium Shows.
- March Break camp.

**Hendervale Stables**
5244 #1 Side Road
R.R. #6
Milton, ON L9T 2Y1
Phone: (905) 827-2234

**Contact:** Janet or Heather Manbert.
**Location:** Northwest of the intersection of Highways 25 and 5.
**Type of Lessons:** English riding lessons. Specialize in hunter/jumper. This stable teaches beginner to intermediate level riders.
**Rates:** Private, semiprivate, and group; thirty-minute private lessons; forty-five-minute semiprivate lessons; one-hour group sessions; special rates for series of six or twelve group lessons; practice sessions. Discounts are offered if there is more than one rider in a family.
**Age Recommendations:** Seven and up. Five- and six-year-olds can take private lessons given by an advanced student at the regular group lesson rate until they are ready to join a group lesson.
**Student Requirements:** Hard hat with welded harness. Shoes or boots with a small heel. Jeans or cords that fit tight to the leg from the knee down.
**Facilities:** Two indoor arenas. Two outdoor jumping fields. Two hundred and fifty acres of hacking trails with about fifty acres of woods. Sixteen school horses, including Thoroughbreds, Thoroughbred types, and grade ponies.
**Instructor Qualifications:** Graduates from Humber College's three-year course, and CEF Level 2 coaching certification.
**Lesson Programs:** Lessons offered Saturdays, 8:00 a.m. to 2:00 p.m.;

Sundays, 3:00 p.m. to 8:00 p.m.; Tuesdays, 5:00 p.m. to 8:00 p.m.; Thursdays, 5:00 p.m. to 8:00 p.m. Students go through a series of nine levels, three at each of the beginner, novice, and intermediate stage. Private, semiprivate, and group lessons. Group maximum is six. Riders sign up for lessons in a series of six or twelve. Make-up lessons are provided if the stable is given more than eight hours notice of a missed lesson.

**Beginners' Programs:** Beginner lessons start with a group of three riders on quiet horses. The instructor is assisted by several helpers. One new rider is added each week until the group has six riders. New riders who are experienced are interviewed about what they've done and put into a group at their estimated level.

**Other Services:**

- Day camps (see listing in Chapter 4).
- Schooling shows from May to October.
- Winter clinics on grooming and show preparation.

**Kilmanagh Valley Farms**
15276 Dixie Road
R.R. #1
Inglewood, ON L0N 1K0
Phone: (905) 584-2116

**Contact:** Mark and Lindsay Grice.

**Location:** At the corner of Olde Base Line and Dixie Road, north of Highway 7 and east of Highway 10.

**Type of Lessons:** Offers everything needed to help riders show on the Quarter Horse circuit. This stable concentrates on horse owners who either want to show their own horses or have professionals show them. Specializes in Hunter Under Saddle, Western Pleasure, Equitation, and Horsemanship. Advanced riders with their own horses can start jumping.

**Rates:** Private and semiprivate lessons; special rates for boarders.

**Age Recommendations:** Six years up to seventy-five. Riders must sign a waiver.

**Student Requirements:** Footwear with a heel. Helmets are optional.

**Facilities:** Indoor arena. Large outdoor sand arena. Round pen. Two lesson horses are used to give new riders the basics while they're looking for their own Quarter Horse.
**Instructor Qualifications:** Successful riders from the A circuit and Quarter Horse circuit.
**Lesson Programs:** Private and semiprivate. Each lesson is geared to the calibre of the riders.
**Beginners' Programs:** Start with the basics of horse handling on the ground before allowing the rider to mount.
**Other Services:**

- Shows on the American Quarter Horse Association Circuit in Ontario and up to the World Champion level in the United States.
- Trailering to more than forty Quarter Horse shows in Ontario each year, and also into the United States.
- Show coaching.
- Video taping.
- Write for a free brochure.

**Meadowlark Stables**
R.R. #2
Streetsville, ON L5M 2B2
Phone: (905) 821-0419

**Location:** Winston Churchill Boulevard just north of Highway 401.
**Type of Lessons:** English riding lessons. This stable specializes in training hunters and jumpers, and dressage riders.
**Rates:** Private, semiprivate, and group lessons; thirty-minute private lessons; semiprivate lessons by special arrangement only; one-hour group lessons; lesson sign-up in groups of four sessions; introductory beginners' package; practice sessions.
**Age Recommendations:** Five and up, depending on the size and attention span of the child.
**Student Requirements:** Boots with a heel. Helmet. Riding crop.
**Facilities:** Two indoor rings, including a hunter ring. Three outdoor rings, including a dressage ring. Jumper field. Has about

thirty ponies and horses of different sizes and temperaments to suit the size and level of the riders.

**Instructor Qualifications:** Experienced riders and coaches.

**Lesson Programs:** Barn office open Monday to Friday, 10:00 a.m. to 9:00 p.m.; Saturdays, 9:00 a.m. to 6:00 p.m.; and Sundays, 10:00 a.m. to 5:00 p.m. Private, semiprivate, and group lessons.

**Beginners' Programs:** Nonriders start with a series of half-hour lessons 1:1 with an instructor. Instruction includes information on grooming and saddling a horse. Riders move to a group within two months. New riders are fit into a class according to their experience. Their level is assessed over the first couple of lessons, and their group is changed if necessary.

**Other Services:**

- Rents helmets and crops.
- Tack shop.
- Riding program for people with disabilities set up as private lessons with volunteer assistants.

**Mobility Riders**
c/o Five Star Ranch
3340 Dundas Street West
Oakville, ON L6J 4Z3
Phone: (905) 827-9578

**Contact:** Kim Bolduc.

**Location:** Dundas Street just west of Highway 25.

**Type of Lessons:** Riding lessons for people with disabilities. Riders must have a doctor's note saying that riding is feasible and rider must be assessed by Kim Bolduc. The type of lesson depends on the disability and number of available volunteers. There are several volunteers per horse.

**Rates:** Price by arrangement.

**Facilities:** Indoor arena. Outdoor arena. Special mounting ramps for people in wheelchairs. Adapted saddles. Some special equipment for people with disabilities. Approximately twenty-four horses.

**Instructor Qualifications:** University degree in Recreational Therapy from the University of Waterloo. Currently working on CEF certification.
**Lesson Programs:** Varies according to need.

**Myrddin**
R.R. #3
Georgetown, ON L7G 4S6
Phone: (905) 877-6698

**Contact:** Margaret or Peter Godson.
**Location:** Nine kilometres north of Highway 401 and west of Trafalgar Road on the south side of the 17th Side Road of Georgetown between the 5th and 6th lines.
**Type of Lessons:** English riding lessons. Specializes in three-day eventing and advanced hunter/jumper.
**Rates:** Private, semiprivate, and group; one hour; introductory package; monthly rate for group lessons.
**Age Recommendations:** Six and up. Younger children are usually started by being led on a pony.
**Student Requirements:** Decent shoes with a heel. Track pants, breeches, or jodhpurs. Helmets mandatory, and can be provided.
**Facilities:** Two indoor arenas. One large outdoor arena. Outdoor jumping ring. Cross-country course. Several water schools. This stable has about twelve school horses of Thoroughbred type and draft cross. There are three ponies.
**Instructor Qualifications:** CEF Level 2 coaching certification. Many years riding and coaching experience. Senior Instructor and Horsemasters' Certificates from Canadian Pony Club 'A'.
**Lesson Programs:** Closed Mondays. Open other days 9:00 a.m. to 9:00 p.m. Private, semiprivate, and group lessons. Group maximum is six. Lessons are flexible in length. If a horse or rider runs into a problem, the lesson will be extended beyond the usual hour. Sign-up is on a monthly basis.
**Beginners' Programs:** Stable has an introductory package of six 1½-hour lessons. These lessons introduce a group of three or

four nonriders to the basics of practical horse handling and riding. Riders who are new to the stable receive an assessment lesson (approximately one hour long), which helps to place them in a group.

**Other Services:**

- Will supply helmets.
- Arranges trailering to events and coaches students through the day.
- Two in-house schooling shows during the winter.

**The Ranch**
5111 Highway 25
R.R. #1
Milton, ON L9T 2X5
Phone: (905) 876-4511

**Location:** On Highway 25 just south of Milton between the Queen Elizabeth Way and Highway 401.
**Type of Lessons:** Western-style lessons in an outdoor ring. The goal of lessons is to teach basic horsemanship. Riders learn to control their own mount during trail rides, with an emphasis on safety.
**Rates:** Hour-long lessons. First private or semiprivate beginner lesson costs the same as the group rate.
**Age Recommendations:** Eight and up.
**Facilities:** The Ranch has twenty-five trail horses, including some ponies and smaller horses of the Quarter Horse and Appaloosa type. Most are quiet.
**Instructor Qualifications:** Variety of qualifications, including CEF certification. Most have grown up enjoying horses. Several have experience with various types of showing, including reining and barrel racing.
**Lesson Programs:** Offers lessons on summer weeknight evenings and winter weekend mornings. Group lessons include five or six students per class. Students sign up for lessons on a weekly basis.
**Beginners' Programs:** Riders receive a private or semiprivate

introductory lesson before they're put into a group.

**Other Services:**

- Riding stables (see listing in Chapter 1) and day camps (see listing in Chapter 4).

**Silver Spring Farm**
1275 Burnhamthorpe Road West
Oakville, ON L4Y 3V7
Phone: (905) 257-0528

**Contact:** Claudia Wagner.
**Location:** On Burnhamthorpe Road west of the Fourth Line.
**Type of Lessons:** English riding lessons. Specializes in show jumpers and hunters. This is a boarding stable that offers some lessons to people who are considering part-boarding a horse or pony.
**Rates:** Private and semiprivate rates.
**Age Recommendations:** Three and up, depending on the individual.
**Student Requirements:** Helmet with fixed safety harness. Paddock boots or a riding boot with a heel. Riding pants or fitted stretch pants.
**Facilities:** Indoor arena. Outdoor sand ring. Flat grass area. Jumps available. Three lesson horses, including a Thoroughbred, and two ponies.
**Instructor Qualifications:** Ridden and shown on the A circuit for nineteen years.
**Lesson Programs:** By appointment. Private and semiprivate. Forty minutes to one hour, depending on what has been accomplished.
**Beginners' Programs:** Nonriders start in private lessons. They are given an introduction in grooming and tacking the horse, as well as in basic horsemanship.
**Other Services:**

- Part-boards horses and ponies.
- Fun show in October.
- Takes students to some schooling shows in spring.
- Coaches and shows on the A circuit.

**Wildwood Manor Ranch**
R.R. #5
Georgetown, ON L7G 4S8
Phone: (905) 877-6852

**Location:** Northeast of the intersection of Trafalgar Road and Highway 7.
**Type of Lessons:** Western lessons with an emphasis on pleasure riding.
**Rates:** Group lessons; one hour. Beginner private lessons are the same rate as group lessons.
**Age Recommendations:** None. Most students are over five years old.
**Student Requirements:** Prefer footwear with a heel or a running shoe, and comfortable loose clothing.
**Facilities:** One hundred acres of varied trails: bush, open fields, rolling country. Very scenic. A learning field with various obstacles. Approximately thirty-five horses.
**Instructor Qualifications:** Humber College graduate and a lot of experience riding.
**Lesson Programs:** Lessons by appointment. Group only. From two to six in a group.
**Beginners' Programs:** Beginners start in private lessons, especially if they are very young. They move to a group when they're ready.
**Other Services:**

- Trail rides (see listing in Chapter 1) and day camps (see listing in Chapter 4).

CHAPTER THREE

# Riding Adventures in Ontario

FOR THOSE WHO AREN'T interested in riding regularly, but like the idea of seeing Ontario the "ride" way, there is a wide variety of vacation packages—one just right for every taste and budget. If you like roughing it, for example, you'll want to choose one of the adventure packages that include overnight camping in a log cabin without power. But if luxury accommodations are more to your taste, why not plan on visiting one of Ontario's many resorts where you can horseback ride during the day but luxuriate in a hot tub at night? There's even horseback riding coupled with dining at one of Canada's top restaurants.

Before choosing a package, of course, you'll want to consider your physical condition. If you do not get some form of energetic exercise on a regular basis, you'll probably be more comfortable with an adventure package that includes a small amount of riding—say an hour or less. On the other hand, if you're an athletic type who enjoys cross-country skiing, aerobic exercise, martial arts, or other physically active sports, you may be interested in one of the longer rides.

Just like any sport, horseback riding should be done with

caution. If you haven't ridden for a year or more, and are planning a horseback adventure that will include more than two hours of riding, take some time to get your body adjusted to the demands of riding. The best way is to go for several one-hour trail rides or take several riding lessons.

You'll also want to make sure that you're dressed for riding. If you don't want to invest in proper riding pants, wear a loose-fitting pair of jeans. Make sure they're large enough to fit comfortably over a pair of long underwear. Like a second pair of socks in hiking boots, the double layer will help protect your legs from painful saddle sores. If you think long underwear will be too hot, then follow the lead of some jockeys and buy a drugstore variety of support hose used by people with varicose veins. Worn under blue jeans, sup-hose offers a lot of leg protection.

Wise clothing choices include boots with a heel. This will prevent your foot from getting caught in the stirrup. If you're a male rider, don't be ashamed to wear an athletic support. Many experienced riders do.

Many adventure riding stables also provide riding helmets. You wouldn't ride a motorcycle or a snowmobile without head protection, would you? Accidents can also happen while horseback riding.

Last, but not least, don't let age prevent you from having fun. Both men and women have learned to ride when in their sixties and older. It is probably a good idea to discuss horseback riding with your doctor as you would before starting any exercise program, and to start slowly.

## RIDING ADVENTURES IN ONTARIO LISTINGS

### *Southern Ontario*

**Cinch Stables Ltd.**
43 Capulet Lane
London, ON N6H 3E6
Phone: (519) 471-3492

**Contact:** Leslie Cornish.
**Location:** South of Highway 22 on Capulet Lane off Oxford Street in London.
**Season:** Year-round. Overnight rides during the summer months. Make reservations. Dates are flexible.
**Rates:** Overnight rides vary in price; check for details.
**Age Recommendations:** None. Children six and under go double with an adult.
**Facilities and Services:** This is a trail riding facility that offers overnight camp-outs that include a two-hour evening ride, sleep-over, and a two-hour ride the next day. Overnights are usually on Friday/Saturday or Saturday/Sunday, and include an evening barbecue and breakfast. Thirty horses. Six ponies. Western saddles. Helmets are available.
**Introduction for Beginners:** Trail guides explain how to turn and stop the horse.
**Trails:** Include a mixture of treed and hilly areas on private and city land.
**Other Services:**

- Day camps (see listing in Chapter 4).

**Circle H Trailrides & Outfitters Ltd.**
349 Alfred Street
Kingston, ON K7K 4H6
Phone: (613) 548-7746

**Contact:** Linda Hunter.

**Location:** North of Highway 401 just southwest of Lyndhurst, forty-five minutes from Kingston.
**Season:** Year-round by reservation.
**Rates:** Hourly riding; special rates for 1 1/2-hour rides; lunch and dinner rides; overnight packages. Write for a free brochure.
**Age Recommendations:** Eight and up. Circle H prefers younger riders to have had a lesson or two before going out on the trail.
**Facilities and Services:** This is a stable that offers trail rides in the bush of the Canadian Shield between Kingston and Ottawa. Offerings include hour and 1 1/2-hour rides, a 2 1/2- to 3-hour lunch ride during which riders eat in the bush, and two different dinner rides. The dinner rides are 2 1/2 to three hours long. Guests choose between chicken breast or steak dinner. Overnight rides for four to ten riders include a camp-out in the bush, evening barbecue, and range-style breakfast. Twenty horses. Only ten to twelve horses take to the trail at one time. Western saddles. No helmets are available.
**Introduction for Beginners:** The trail guide goes over the riding basics when the riders get on. These basics include showing people how to hold and use the reins, and the correct position for their feet while the horse is climbing hills. Trail guides stop before each hill and review the proper position before starting to climb. Trail guides are particularly patient with riders who are frightened of horses. They will work with such riders in a fenced corral until they feel confident to go out on the trail.
**Trails:** Hilly wooded areas of the Canadian Shield. Some trails pass beaver ponds and travel through meadows.
**Other Services:**

- Birthday outings and special "Kid Activity" days.
- Camping in nearby Charleston Lake Provincial Park.
- Rental accommodation nearby.
- Hay rides and sleigh rides.

**Circle R Ranch**
Box 85
Delaware, ON N0L 1E0
Phone: (519) 471-3799

**Contact:** Rick Romman.
**Location:** On Delaware Concession 2, which is two kilometres north of Highway 2, eight kilometres west of London.
**Season:** Spring and fall for morning rides and brunches.
**Rates:** Special low rate for a trail ride with lunch.
**Age Recommendations:** Eight and up. Younger children can ride a pony led by an adult who is not riding.
**Facilities and Services:** This is a trail riding facility that offers two morning rides and three afternoon rides during weekends. One ride leaves at 10:00 a.m. followed by a brunch of pancakes, salads, coffee, and juice. The second ride leaves at 11:30 a.m. preceded by brunch. The afternoon rides are at 1:00 p.m., 2:30 p.m., and 4:00 p.m. The stable has more than forty horses and ten ponies. Western saddles. No helmets are available.
**Introduction for Beginners:** With groups, the trail guides provide a ten- to fifteen-minute lesson on horse management basics, which includes a brief lesson on how to stop and turn a horse.
**Trails:** Two hundred acres of open pasture and hardwood forest.
**Other Services:**

- Day camps (see listing in Chapter 4).
- Hay and sleigh rides by arrangement. During the spring, these can be organized with tours of a working sugar bush.
- Write for a free brochure.

**Country Rose Ranch**
10961 Neff Road
R.R. #2
Port Colborne, ON  L3K 5V4
Phone: (905) 835-8768

**Contact:** Cathy Warren or Mike Paterson.
**Location:** Neff Road off Highway 3 just outside Port Colborne. A second summer location at Sherkstone Shores Park, eleven kilometres east of Port Colborne on Highway 3.
**Season:** May to September.
**Rates:** Ride and breakfast, and sunset ride with campfire/wiener roast cost the same.
**Age Recommendations:** Eight and up.
**Facilities and Services:** Trail riding and Western lessons. Rides include a one-hour breakfast ride along the Lake Erie beach followed by a ranch-style breakfast in a nearby park restaurant. Sunset rides include a beach ride followed by a campfire, wiener roast, and singsong. About ten horses, including ones large enough for heavy riders. Western saddles. No helmets are available.
**Introduction for Beginners:** Beginners are instructed in how to ride on the trail. Complete beginners are advised to take a one-hour lesson before the trail ride. All rides are guided.
**Trails:** Through bush and along the Lake Erie shore.
**Other Services:**

- Lessons for beginners to advanced.
- Specializes in training reining horses.
- Hay and sleigh rides for groups.
- Boarding facility with indoor arena.
- Regular students from the school can take out a horse on their own.
- Overnight rides and camp-outs by arrangement.

**Ganaraska Ranch**
R.R. #3
Pontypool, ON L0A 1K0
Phone: (705) 277-1810

**Contact:** Peter Brackett.
**Location:** Just off Highway 15, east of Pontypool.
**Season:** Year-round.
**Rates:** Hourly rates; weekend riding package with meals; riders get special rate on renting a cabin that sleeps four.
**Age Recommendations:** Eight and up for hourly riding. Twelve and up for the weekend ride. Children under sixteen must be accompanied by an adult.
**Facilities and Services:** This is a stable that offers trail rides, lessons, and weekend outings. The weekend adventures run from Friday afternoon to Sunday afternoon. On Friday, there's a one-hour lesson and a two-hour trail ride followed by a late dinner and bonfire. Saturday starts with a ranch breakfast followed by a four-hour ride, a lunch break, and a second four-hour ride followed by a steak dinner, bonfire, and entertainment. On Sunday, there's a light breakfast, four-hour ride, and brunch. Riders can camp right on the property or rent a cabin for the weekend. Twenty-five trail horses, including some ponies and smaller horses. Most are quiet. Western saddles. Helmets are available.
**Introduction for Beginners:** The one-hour lesson on Friday gives riders an introduction on handling their trail horse.
**Trails:** Ganaraska Forest, which is a large tract of Crown Land with many scenic logging trails. Riders frequently see wildlife, including deer, coyotes, raccoons, rabbits, and wild turkeys.
**Other Services:**

- Cabin accommodation available at inexpensive rates.
- Riders can bring their own tent or trailer.
- Some Saturday evening hoedowns.
- Moonlight rides with food, music, and campfire.
- Full-day rides with lunch.

**Harbourfront Adventure Travel Club**
283A Queen's Quay West
Toronto, ON M5V 1A2
Phone: (416) 203-2277

**Contact:** Darryl Gould or Scott Kerby.
**Season:** Fall.
**Rates:** Vary depending on package.
**Facilities and Services:** This is a club that offers trail riding and camping. It makes arrangements with various stables in southern and central Ontario, and develops riding packages that include transportation from Toronto. Offerings include day trips to stables near Toronto and overnight trail rides farther afield. Trips change on a regular basis. Call for specifics. Western saddles.

**Lazy Acre Farm**
R.R. #3
Allenford, ON N0H 1A0
Phone: (519) 935-2957

**Contact:** Dieter VonRichter.
**Location:** Just east of Highway 6 and west of Owen Sound.
**Season:** May to October.
**Rates:** Regular rates for one-hour trail rides; special rates for longer rides; special riding rates for people who rent the farm's housekeeping cabin for one week (Saturday to Friday).
**Age Recommendations:** Prefer riders ten and up. Younger children may ride if they have previous experience.
**Facilities and Services:** This is a trail riding stable and working farm with cabins. The VonRichters breed Morgan horses. They break and train a variety of horses for Western-style riders. The farm also has exotic animals. Rides are one to 2 1/2 hours long, depending on the skill of the riders. Thirty horses, including two ponies and two small donkeys for pony rides. Western saddles. No helmets.
**Introduction for Beginners:** While they help the riders mount,

trail guides explain how to sit on a horse, how to stay on, and how to hold and use the reins. All rides are supervised.

**Trails:** Through rolling hills and bush trails. Most are at a leisurely pace.

**Other Services:**

- Housekeeping cabin that includes everything but the food, soap, and towels. Riding rate reductions for people who rent the cabin.
- Some bed-and-breakfast accommodation.

**The Mansfield Guest Ranch**

P.O. Box 76
Mansfield, ON L0N 1M0
Phone: (705) 435-5885 or 1-800-361-9591.

**Contact:** Tracey Hepburn.

**Location:** Six minutes north of Airport Road and Highway 89.

**Season:** May to October.

**Rates:** Hourly rides; overnight and day packages; produces customized packages for groups of six to forty clients. Write for the free brochure and rate list.

**Age Recommendations:** Ten and up. Will supervise young children and give them pony rides during adult outings.

**Facilities and Services:** Overnight adult and family accommodation with emphasis on educating guests about how animals serve people, improving human-animal communication, and providing a healthy and nutritious holiday. Weekend package includes a 6:00 p.m. Friday arrival, campfire, one-hour horsemanship workshop, and social hour. Saturday includes a hearty ranch breakfast, lunch, buffet dinner, forty-minute riding lesson, two two-hour rides, line dancing in the hayloft studio, and some free time. Sunday is similar to Saturday, minus the evening entertainment. More than two hundred horses, many of Quarter Horse type. No more than six to ten riders on the trail at one time. Western. Helmets are available and mandatory for those sixteen and under.

**Introduction for Beginners:** All guests receive a forty-minute lesson on the basics of horse handling.
**Trails:** Niagara Escarpment.
**Other Services:**

- Swimming pool, volleyball, baseball, trout fishing, and hiking.

**North Ridge Farm**
R.R. #2
Baden, ON N0B 1G0
Phone: (519) 634-8595

**Contact:** Sarah Banbury.
**Location:** Ten minutes from Kitchener, north of Highway 7.
**Season:** Year-round.
**Rates:** Bed-and-breakfast with additional meals by arrangement; separate rates for individual guests and couples; guests can take private lessons from the owner or one of her advanced students.
**Age Recommendations:** No preference. Younger children taught by advanced students at a lower rate.
**Facilities and Services:** This is a lesson stable that offers bed-and-breakfast accommodation for people who would like to come for weekend riding. The instructor has her CEF Level 1 coaching. She is a recognized CEF judge for hunter/jumper and dressage, and has been teaching riding for more than thirty years. Private English lessons. Basic and dressage. Length varies depending on what has been accomplished. Indoor arena. Outdoor dressage ring. Some jumps and cross-country fences. Riders should wear a helmet and shoes or boots with a heel. Six horses of mixed breeds used in the riding school.
**Introduction for Beginners:** Beginners are started on a longe line. Emphasis is on getting them up and posting. A small amount of stable management is taught to adult beginners. Child beginners are taught by an advanced student in the school. These lessons start with an introduction to basic horsemanship.
**Other Services:**

- Will loan hard hats with a harness.

- Bed-and-breakfast.
- "Pony play week" for children aged four to twelve during the summer. This is an introduction to horses and ponies.

**Riding Centre at Horseshoe Valley**
Box 50, Horseshoe Valley
R.R. #1
Barrie, ON L4M 4Y8
Phone: (705) 835-3006

**Contact:** Reta Regelink.
**Location:** Oro Concession 4 just south of Horseshoe Valley Road.
**Season:** May 24 to Thanksgiving.
**Rates:** Hourly rates for trail riding; special pony-ride rates; group rates for hay and sleigh rides.
**Age Recommendations:** Seven and up. Adults can rent a pony and take younger children for a ten-minute ride.
**Facilities and Services:** Trail riding. Take a nature walk on horseback during your weekend stay at Horseshoe Valley. Family-oriented. About ten horses. Western saddles. Helmets available.
**Introduction for Beginners:** Trail guides explain how to manoeuvre a horse. All trail rides are guided by experienced guides.
**Trails:** Flat bush trails with sandy footing.
**Other Services:**

- Hay and sleigh rides.
- Pony rides.
- Specialty carriage rides.

**Rocky Ridge Ranch**
R.R. #2
Rockwood, ON N0B 2K0
Phone: (905) 854-2584

**Contact:** Bill Chapman.

**Location:** North of Highway 401 between Highway 25 and Guelph Line.
**Season:** Spring and fall.
**Rates:** Overnight ride with three meals and use of facilities for the day. Check for current rates.
**Age Recommendations:** Nine and up on horses. Children under nine can ride a pony in the ring. If they seem capable of handling it, they can take it out on the trail.
**Facilities and Services:** This is a trail riding and riding camp facility that offers overnight bunkhouse accommodation. The overnight package includes breakfast, a morning ride, lunch, an afternoon ride, and dinner. Groups of ten only. Smaller groups can be fit together. No alcoholic beverages are allowed on the site. Fifty-eight horses, including about ten ponies. Western saddles. No helmets are available.
**Introduction for Beginners:** Every ride includes a ten- to fifteen-minute introductory session on how to mount, dismount, turn, and stop a horse. Riders have time to practice their skills in the ring before heading out on the trail.
**Trails:** Rolling and wooded hills of the Niagara Escarpment.
**Other Services:**

- Riding stable (see listing in Chapter 1).
- One-day and overnight school bookings during the fall and spring.

**Sauble Trails**
c/o Blain Lewis
R.R. #3
Tara, ON N0H 2N0
Phone: (519) 934-2113 (home), (519) 934-2310 (barn)

**Contact:** Blain Lewis or Betty MacAloney.
**Location:** Off Highway 21 between Allenford and Southampton.
**Season:** Year-round.
**Rates:** Rates for one-hour to all-day rides.
**Age Recommendations:** Prefer riders at least five years old and

up. Children must ride their own mount and have to be tall enough for their feet to fit into the stirrups. There are special children-sized stirrups that fit some saddles.
**Facilities and Services:** This is a trail riding establishment that can accommodate overnight camping. All-day rides and overnight camping are by arrangement only. A group of ten is needed for these rides. Thirty-two grade horses that simply follow the horse in front of them and are safe for beginning riders. Western saddles. Helmets are available.
**Introduction for Beginners:** Trail guides show riders how to stop and turn a horse.
**Trails:** Wooded trails and rolling hills.
**Other Services:**

- Hay rides by arrangement.

**Southbreeze**
R.R. #1
Locust Hill, ON  L0H 1J0
Phone: (905) 472-8224

**Contact:** Christine or Brian Murphy.
**Location:** Five kilometres west of Brock Road on Highway 7.
**Open:** June, July, August, September.
**Rates:** Flat rate per person for weekend trail riding; includes food, horse, equipment, and guide for Friday to Sunday.
**Age Recommendations:** Seven and up.
**Facilities and Services:** Camping and trail riding stable with a special weekend package. On Friday, riders drive to a good campsite about two hours away from Toronto. They have a late dinner, an introduction to the horses, and a short evening ride. After Saturday breakfast, riders are on the trail at 10:00 a.m. They eat a packed lunch on the trail, then return to the campsite around 3:00 p.m. for a rest before the evening barbecue dinner, campfire, and singsong. Sunday includes a breakfast, two-hour ride, and camp lunch. Guests break camp by 3:00 p.m. Trail rides are mainly at a walk and trot; some canters for experienced

riders. Handles up to eight riders per weekend. Two guides per group. Western saddles. Helmets are mandatory for children sixteen and under.

**Trails:** Varies.

**Other Services:**

- Riding lessons (see listing in Chapter 2).
- Week-long ride to the United States planned two or three times per year.

**Talisman Mountain Resort**
Kimberley, ON N0C 1G0
Phone: (519) 599-2520 or (416) 364-0061

**Contact:** Rainer Pommer/Hotel Manager, or Walker Stables (see listing in Chapter 4).

**Location:** Off Highway 10 south of Meaford.

**Season:** May to November.

**Rates:** Special hourly rates for resort guests.

**Age Recommendations:** Six and up.

**Facilities and Services:** This is a year-round holiday resort that includes trail riding among many other on-site activities. Guests can take one-hour trail rides on one of six horses guided by experienced trail guides. Western saddles. No helmets available.

**Introduction for Beginners:** All Talisman guests can have a thirty-minute to one-hour introductory session that includes how to groom, mount, and direct a horse. This introductory session is done on the ground at some point before the arranged trail ride.

**Trails:** Horses climb scenic ski hills in the beautiful Beaver Valley and explore this area.

**Other Services:**

- Weekend getaways with resort accommodation. Includes riding as part of a luxury package or as a day's outing with dinner.

## *Central Ontario*

**Blue Ridge Riding Stables**
R.R. #3
Collingwood, ON L9Y 3Z2
Phone: (705) 445-7105

**Location:** On Osler Bluff Road between Collingwood and Blue Mountain.
**Season:** Year-round, weather permitting.
**Rates:** Rates for one- and two-hour rides; overnight rides by arrangement for groups of at least six; group rates for hay and sleigh rides.
**Age Recommendations:** Eight and up. Children must be tall enough for their feet to fit into the stirrups. Smaller and younger children are encouraged to ride a pony in a corral.
**Facilities and Services:** This is a trail riding stable. One- and two-hour trail rides. Hay and sleigh rides. Nine horses of Quarter Horse type. Western. Helmets are available and must be worn by those under sixteen years of age.
**Introduction for Beginners:** Trail guides spend several minutes showing riders what to do. All rides are at a walk.
**Trails:** Very scenic bush.
**Other Services:**

- Overnight rides by arrangement for groups of six.

**Harmony Acres**
R.R. #1
Tobermory, ON N0H 2R0
Phone: (519) 596-2735

**Contact:** Laurie Adams.
**Location:** On Highway 6 about five kilometres south of Tobermory.
**Season:** May to October. Other times by request. Make reservations during the summer and for the longer rides.
**Rates:** Hourly, two-hour, three-hour rides, and cave trips; half-

and full-day rides with lunch.
**Age Recommendations:** Eight and up. Younger riders are assessed and may ride at the discretion of Harmony Acres owners. No riding double allowed.
**Facilities and Services:** This is a trail riding stable that offers one-hour trail rides as well as Georgian Bay package rides that include two- and three-hour rides to the shore. The cave trip is a two-hour ride and hike to explore a hidden cave. Riders can see Georgian Bay from a scenic lookout. Half- and full-day rides include lunch. Fourteen horses. Western saddles. Helmets available.
**Introduction for Beginners:** Everyone gets a brief ten- to fifteen-minute introductory lesson. Depending on their experience and ability, customers can take a half-hour lesson before the trail ride.
**Trails:** Scenic trails along the Georgian Bay shoreline. Includes wooded and cliff sections. Bear, deer, and grouse are occasionally spotted.
**Other Services:**

- Campground facilities in a hardwood bush with twenty-five sites.
- Small travel trailer rentals.
- Fine dining restaurant rated as one of the top 500 in Canada in 1992.
- Will arrange lunch packages for riders.

**Lakeview Stables**
R.R. #3
Port Carling, ON P0B 1J0
Phone: (705) 765-3513

**Contact:** Pam Braybrook.
**Location:** Eight kilometres north of Bala off Highway 169.
**Season:** Year-round, weather permitting.
**Rates:** One- and two-hour rides; Sunday riding club; fifteen-minute pony rides.
**Age Recommendations:** Eight and up. No riding double. Younger children may go for a fifteen- to thirty-minute pony

ride in the kiddie corral.

**Facilities and Services:** This is a trail riding stable that offers both English and Western lessons and has a summer day camp. One- and two-hour trail rides. The longer ones are for the more experienced riders. A Sunday adult riding club teaches beginners a little about horses before they go for a ride. About fifty horses. Western and English saddles.

**Introduction for Beginners:** Trail guides spend about ten minutes showing clients how to mount, dismount, and hold their feet in the stirrups. Emphasis is on safety. Beginners use Western saddles.

**Trails:** Mostly bush, some flat stretches.

**Other Services:**

- Day camps (see listing in Chapter 4).
- Lessons.
- Riding for people with disabilities. The stable works by arrangement with riders who are blind, deaf, or have an intellectual disability.

**Laurentian Lodge and Outdoor Centre**

Box 250
Dorset, ON P0A 1E0
Phone: (705) 766-9320

**Contact:** Greg Rushton.

**Location:** About twelve kilometres off Highway 35, about twelve kilometres southeast of Dorset.

**Season:** Early May to mid-October.

**Rates:** Hourly riding; ride and breakfast; ride and lunch; ride and dinner; overnight ride.

**Age Recommendations:** Seven and up on the trail. Younger children are led at a walk in a fenced corral.

**Facilities and Services:** This is a lodge with both cabin or lodge accommodation complete with hot tubs, a sauna, and excellent dining. The lodge provides many sporting and learning activities, including hourly horseback rides and lessons. Guests can take a horse to breakfast at a wilderness lake, arrange for a packed lunch and ride, or enjoy a dinner ride that features a gourmet meal with stuffed rainbow trout, eaten beside an isolated lake. Overnight rides explore a wilderness area. Riders stay overnight in heated tents or cabins. A great place for listening to the wolves. English or Western saddles. Helmets are available and mandatory. Riders must also wear boots with a heel.

**Introduction for Beginners:** Guests interested in riding are given a lesson that emphasizes riding as a partnership between the horse and rider. Before an overnight ride, guests go for a short trail ride to evaluate their comfort level with the horse and their ability to handle it. They are coached in how to direct their mount.

**Trails:** Nearly 50,000 acres of Crown Land with logging roads, rolling highland forest, and isolated lakes.

**Other Services:**

- Dog sledding, cross-country skiing, and kayaking.
- Painting, photography, and native programs.
- Corporate adventure programs.
- Youth at risk programs.
- Caters to religious groups and offers vegetarian meals if requested.

**Oxbow Ranch**
R.R. #6
Bracebridge, ON P0B 1C0
Phone: (705) 385-2848

**Contact:** Ed Bilz or Marilyn LaRose.

**Location:** Fifteen kilometres north and west of Bracebridge off Muskoka Road 4 on Beatrice Townline.

**Season:** May 1 to the end of November.

**Rates:** Hourly and all-day rides; two-day wilderness pack trips; four-hour cattle roundups with a chuckwagon dinner; buggy rides. Write for a price list and brochure.

**Age Recommendations:** Ten and up. Riders must fit into an adult-sized saddle.

**Facilities and Services:** This is a trail riding establishment where young horses are broken and trained, and pack trips offered. Oxbow Ranch offers a variety of pack trips, all with two wranglers per ride. Overnight rides include a 48-kilometre trip and bunkhouse accommodation located in the bush away from all the modern amenities. Great for people who want to get back to nature. The evening meal is a steak barbecue cooked in an open pit. Twenty-two good saddle horses. One pony for rent to adults who want to lead a child around the corral. Western saddles. No helmets are available.

**Introduction for Beginners:** As the riders are helped on their horses, the trail guide offers suggestions on turning and stopping the horse. During the ride, one of the trail guides stops and explains how to handle each trail obstacle such as a steep hill or stream. If advanced and novice riders are in the same group, the party will split at some sections so that the more advanced riders can enjoy a controlled canter or lope.

**Trails:** Lots of hills, streams, and open areas.

**Other Services:**

- Will work with riders with disabilities on a call-ahead basis. Such riders can be given a controlled ride in a round corral. If riders have extreme disabilities, trail guides will ask help from the people accompanying the rider.
- Ask about longer pack trips and cattle round-ups that include a four-hour ride and chuckwagon lunch.
- Group and private Western riding lessons.
- Team penning club.

**Stewart Coughlin Riding Ranch**

Box 476
South River, ON  P0A 1X0
Phone: (705) 386-7465

**Contact:** Anyone who answers the phone.

**Location:** West of Highway 11 at South River.

**Season:** Year-round.
**Rates:** Half-hour, one-, two-, and three-hour rides; half-day and all-day trail rides; flexible times; group sleigh rides; competitive rates.
**Age Recommendations:** None. Three-year-old children have been out on trail rides. Some younger children ride double with their parents. At other times, children ride their own horse, which is led by a lead line.
**Facilities and Services:** This is a trail riding and lesson establishment that will make special arrangements for people who would like to come and stay nearby and arrange day or half-day rides. Riders can also camp on the property. Fifteen trail horses, most of them raised on the ranch. Three Shetland ponies. Western or English saddles. No helmets are available.
**Introduction for Beginners:** Trail guides, most of whom include members of the Coughlin family, show riders how to hold, adjust, and handle their reins. They give instructions from the time riders leave the hitching rack until they return. This allows the stable to make sure that its horses are properly ridden. It also means that all horses will do what the rider tells them instead of simply following the horse in front.
**Trails:** One hundred and twenty-five acres of rough bush pasture typical of the Canadian Shield. Rolling hills, creeks, fields, streams, and a maple bush—fabulously scenic. Deer and partridge are frequently seen during rides.
**Other Services:**

- Riding facilities for people with physical disabilities. There is a ramp to allow riders to mount from a wheelchair.
- Camping on the property. Camping and motel accommodation nearby.
- Sleigh rides include a snack of hot chocolate, hot cider, and cookies.
- Public washrooms, including facilities for people with physical disabilities.

**Sunrise Stables**
Box 32
Port Severn, ON L0K 1S0
Phone: (705) 756-2142

**Contact**: Donna Welsh.
**Location:** Off Muskoka Road 34, east of Highway 69.
**Season:** Year-round; peak is May 24 to Labour Day.
**Rates:** One-hour and 1 1/2-hour rides; sleigh rides.
**Age Recommendations:** Three and up. Younger children may ride double by sitting on the saddle in front of a parent. Such rides are at a walk only.
**Facilities and Services:** This is a trail riding stable that specializes in family and seniors' outings. Many rides are done solely at a walk to make them safer for these groups. Sunrise Stables offers one- and 1 1/2-hour trail rides as well as winter group sleigh rides. Sleigh rides include a bonfire and cookout. Twenty to thirty quiet trail mounts. There are smaller horses for children. Western saddles.
**Introduction for Beginners:** Many trail rides are at a walk because this is the safest gait for beginners. Nonriders are given a five-minute introductory lesson during which they're shown how to mount, adjust their stirrups, sit properly, hold the reins, and turn the horse. They are advised to keep their toes in the stirrups.
**Trails:** Canadian Shield scenery, including rocky areas, wooded trails, and some fields.
**Other Services:**

- Day camps (see listing in Chapter 4).
- Fall colour rides.

**Wild Echo Lodge**
P.O. Box 17
Port Stanton, ON P0E 1N0
Phone: (705) 689-6388 or 1-800-461-8917

**Contact:** Doug Stanton.
**Location:** Twenty-four kilometres northwest of Orillia and west

of Highway 11.

**Season:** July to October.

**Rates:** Special outdoor adventure package with lower rates in the fall; regular rates during summer months.

**Age Recommendations:** By assessment.

**Facilities and Services:** This is a lodge with horseback riding packages. In the off-season, it provides horseback riding adventures for clientele. The outdoor adventure includes a horse grooming and tack clinic, a one-hour trail ride, and a boat and motor pass to allow guests to explore the Trent-Severn Waterway. Approximately six horses. Western. Helmets are mandatory.

**Introduction for Beginners:** Before riding, lodge guests receive a riding clinic about the dos and don'ts of trail riding.

**Trails:** 16,000 acres of Crown Land in the rugged Canadian Shield.

**Other Services:**

- Other riding packages being developed.
- Water skiing, tennis, supervised children's program, complete lodge and dining facilities.

**Woodrow Farm**

R.R. #1
Balderson, ON  K0G 1A0
Phone: (613) 267-1493

**Contact:** Ann Miller.

**Location:** North of Highway 7 near Balderson, eight kilometres north of Perth.

**Season:** May to November. Bed-and-breakfast facilities open year-round.

**Rates:** Special horse-lover's weekend; includes accommodation, two breakfasts, two lunches, two dinners, and two trail rides.

**Age Recommendations:** None if the person has previous riding experience. Ten and up for novices.

**Facilities and Services:** This is a vacation farm and bed-and-breakfast facility located in the Ottawa Valley. The owners offer trail riding to guests ten-years-old and over. Special attention is

given to guests who do not have previous riding experience. All rides are escorted by an experienced leader, and the horses are well-mannered and quiet. Trail rides are geared to the interest and ability of the rider. Four horses. English or Western saddles. Helmets must be worn, and will be provided if necessary.
**Introduction for Beginners:** Complete beginners are led. All rides are geared to the level of the house guests.
**Trails:** Scenic trails around the Ottawa Valley.
**Other Services:**

- Bed-and-bales (accommodation for both horse and rider). Horse must have a negative Coggins Test. Guests may wish to trail ride during their stay, or use this service while transporting horses through the area.

## *Northern Ontario*

### Cedar Rail Ranch

R.R. #3
Thessalon, ON  P0R 1L0
Phone: (705) 842-2021

**Contact:** Cathy Jarratt.
**Location:** Off Highway 17 about twenty-four kilometres north of Thessalon on Highway 129.
**Season:** May to October for overnights. Year-round for the rest of the facility.
**Rates:** Two-hour rides; day trips with lunch; discount for three or more in a group; overnight trail rides; 10 per cent discount for groups of six; hay and sleigh rides; housekeeping cabins by the night or week.
**Age Recommendations:** Twelve and up for overnight rides. The ranch suggests that younger children should be avid riders with previous riding experience.
**Facilities and Services:** This is a trail riding stable that offers a small number of lessons for local riders. The ranch has an overnight riding business and housekeeping cabins that can accommodate

riders who would like to vacation there and ride out on a regular basis. Overnight rides are Friday to Sunday. On Friday, the guests ride for 1 1/2 hours to the outpost camp where they spend the weekend on the shore of Tunnel Lake. Saturday can include a day ride or shorter excursions, depending on the group. The group can be split if riders want different amounts of riding. There is an evening barbecue and access to a boat and motor, or a canoe. Sunday is a lazy day with a sleep-in and short trail ride or beach holiday. Riding plans are flexible according to the needs and desires of the group. Guests are back at the ranch by 1:00 p.m. Six horses. Western saddles. Helmets are offered.

**Introduction for Beginners:** All trail rides and overnights begin with a short introductory lesson that includes the safety basics: how to mount, dismount, turn, and stop.

**Trails:** A mixture of bush trails, sand, and creek typical of the Canadian Shield.

**Other Services:**

- Nonriders can stay at the outpost camp with the riders.
- Hay and sleigh rides.
- Housekeeping cabins by the night or week.
- Trout fishing pond.
- Write for a free brochure.

**Double DD Ranch**

R.R. #2
Cumberland, ON K0A 1S0
Phone: (613) 833-2317

**Location:** Highway 17 East between Cumberland and Rockland, about twenty minutes from downtown Ottawa.

**Season:** Year-round. Saturday and Sunday, 9 a.m. to 5 p.m.

**Age Recommendations:** Eight and up. About 90 per cent of the customers are children. For them, the ranch has good quiet horses.

**Facilities and Services:** This is a trail riding stable that offers hourly riding as well as hay and sleigh rides. No reservations

necessary, but experienced riders should come in the morning when it isn't as busy. Western or English.
**Trails:** Bush trails through private property.
**Other Services:**

- Day camp (see listing in Chapter 4).
- Hall for indoor get-togethers and bean suppers.
- Group barbecues and office picnics.
- Barn dances.
- Weddings.
- Cross-country skiing and tobogganing.

**Pinto Valley Ranch**
Fitzroy Harbour, ON  K0A 1X0
Phone: (613) 623-3439

**Contact:** Ernie Smith.
**Location:** Thirty minutes drive west of Ottawa on Galetta Side Road.
**Season:** Year-round.
**Rates:** Hourly and overnight trail rides; hay and sleigh rides; reasonable rates.
**Age Recommendations:** Depends on ability. Nonriders are started in a corral and offered a lesson if they appear nervous. Children can ride on the trail if they have taken lessons and can control a horse.
**Facilities and Services:** This is a trail riding stable that offers hourly and overnight trail rides. The overnight includes five hours of riding, a steak dinner, sleepover, and hay ride. Most are held on Friday nights or during the week by arrangement. About one hundred horses. Western or English saddles.
**Introduction for Beginners:** Trail rides begin with a few quick pointers on how to ride. The trail guide explains position and control along the trail.
**Trails:** Scenic trails through the bush.
**Other Services:**

- Weddings.

- Company picnics.
- Petting zoo.
- Lessons.
- Hay and sleigh rides.
- Birthday parties.

**Silver Birches Resort**
R.R. #1
Little Current, ON P0P 1K0
Phone: (705) 368-2669

**Contact:** Bill or Betty Ferguson.
**Location:** Manitoulin Island, twenty minutes from Little Current.
**Season:** May 24 to Thanksgiving.
**Rates:** Resort stay with hourly riding or a riding package; special weekend tour with special rate for those who supply their own transportation from southern Ontario; guests also flown in from southern Ontario.
**Age Recommendations:** Five and over. This is usually left up to the parent. Younger children are encouraged to take a twenty-minute pony ride.
**Facilities and Services:** This is a vacation resort that offers hourly horseback riding to guests. There is also a weekend riding tour that includes a Friday to Sunday stay and an overnight riding trip. Thirty horses. Western saddles. Helmets are available and mandatory for those under the age of eighteen.
**Introduction for Beginners:** Trail guides give a brief introduction to horseback riding etiquette before each trail ride. Most of the ride is at a walk. Some trotting, depending on the experience of the group.
**Trails:** Wooded hill country. The trail climbs towards a lookout tower overlooking the North Channel.
**Other Services:**

- Full resort package.

Many riding lesson stables also teach the students the proper technique of saddling and bridling a horse.

Proper English riding apparel. Many stables will allow beginner students to wear jeans and rain boots until they are more advanced.

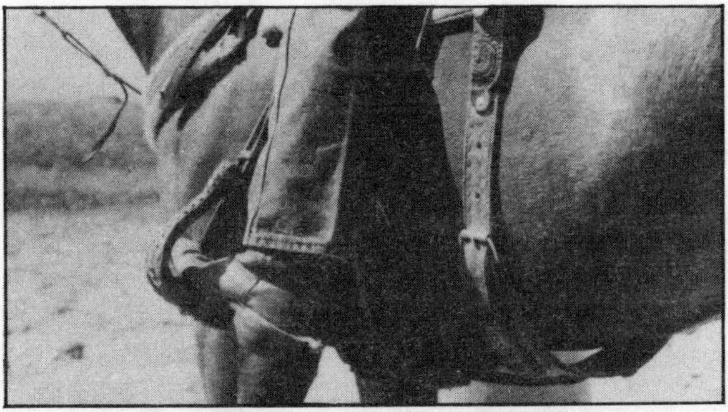

Western riding boots have a heel designed to keep the rider's foot from slipping through the stirrup.

Jumping a fence in the hunter pony division of the Royal Winter Fair.

These students enrolled in a horse management and riding course at an Ontario community college are learning how to exercise race horses.

Fording a stream. Most horseback adventurers would never attempt water this deep. *Almaguin Trail Rides.*

Pack horses are often used to bring supplies into isolated campsites.

Horseback vacations can be enjoyed by people of all ages.

Safety precautions include wearing a proper helmet and boots, as well as checking that the saddle's girth is still tight after a few minutes of riding.

Many riding camps throughout Ontario offer horseback riding vacations for young people.

Driving is another equine sport that appeals to many people.

CHAPTER FOUR

# Riding Camps

ASK HORSE LOVERS AND they'll tell you that riding a horse is great—but spending extended periods with the same horse is even better. That's where residential and day riding camps come to the rescue of those parents who can't afford to buy and care for a family horse.

Close to Metropolitan Toronto and other urban areas, there are many riding stables that offer summer, March Break, and even Christmas Week day camps for riders who want to improve their skills. During the summer, keen riders can also choose from among a variety of day and residential camps that concentrate on a number of horse activities.

For children who are interested in going away to a camp and like horses, but may not want to spend the whole day around them, residential camps throughout Ontario offer a variety of riding programs—everything from a horse lover's package to sports camps where weekly or biweekly riding is part of a general program.

When looking at residential camps, consider the needs and desires of your child or children. Do they have experience staying away from home? If not, you may want to send them on a couple of overnight trips to see how they handle being away from their family. If they aren't emotionally ready for this type of separation, it's better to forget about residential camp and opt for one of the many day facilities.

Residential camps have varying amounts of horse-related activities. The one you choose will depend on a number of things: your child's wishes, your wishes, and your pocketbook.

Children and young teens who read every horse book they can get their hands on and who collect anything with even the slightest touch of horsiness would probably be very happy at a horse camp. Whether or not they are beginners, such children long for the sight, sound, and smell of horses. I know because I was one of them. One week with a horse—any horse—was, and still is, my idea of heaven.

For children who don't have quite that intensity of interest, you may want to choose a camp that has a general riding program or riding option coupled with a sports or outdoor program. Consider this a test. If your child comes home talking of nothing but horses, look for a horse camp the next time. On the other hand, you may have a child who enjoys other activities as well as riding.

Consider whether your child really wants a riding experience. Also consider how competitive your child is. If he or she loves competing, you may wish to look for one of the camps that offers a horse show or other competition at the end of camp. For those who prefer to work without competition, more and more camps now feature end-of-camp exhibitions that demonstrate what children have learned without pitting them one against the other. You may also be interested in the many facilities that don't have either a horse show or demonstration, but simply concentrate on providing children with an enjoyable and safe experience with horses.

If you are an adult who wanted to go to riding camp but never had the chance, take a look at the following listings: Walker Stables, Fieldstone Farm, Ostler Park Equestrian Centre, The Horse People Inc., and The Peterson Woods Outdoor Centre. All of these riding camps welcome adult clients.

## DAY CAMP LISTINGS

### *Inside Metro Toronto*

**Claireville Day Camp**
c/o Etobicoke Parks & Recreation Services
Etobicoke City Hall
399 The West Mall
Etobicoke, ON M9C 2Y2
Phone: (416) 394-8546

**Contact:** Kerrie Lumley.
**Location:** Claireville Conservation Area near Highway 50 and Steeles.
**Season:** July and August. Monday to Friday, 9:15 a.m. to 4:00 p.m. Children are picked up in Etobicoke starting at 8:15 a.m. and dropped off by 5:30 p.m.
**Rates:** Nine- and ten-day sessions; nine-day sessions occur around long weekends.
**Age Recommendations:** Ages 10–14.
**Camp Program:** Day camp. Western. Provides a safe introduction to riding as a pleasurable hobby. Emphasis is on having fun with horses. Half-day of riding, weather permitting. Combines lessons and trail rides. Includes overnight trail ride and camp-out. Handles novice to intermediate riders. Evaluations at each level. Helmets mandatory and can be rented. Riders also require boots with a heel and long pants. Beginners are grouped together. The other riders are divided into groups according to their age and level.
**Instructor Qualifications:** CEF Level 1 coach. Experience working with youth. Horseback riding skills.

**Redstone Farm**
R.R. #1
Richmond Hill, ON L4C 4X7
Phone: (905) 884-2555

**Contact:** Stable manager.

**Location:** On Elgin Mills East, just north of Major MacKenzie Drive between Bayview and Highway 404. Ten-minute walk from Richmond Hill via Bayview bus stop.
**Season:** July.
**Rates:** One- and two-week sessions; reduction for children entered in two two-week sessions and for two children from the same family in any two-week session; price break for those providing their own transportation; helmet rentals. Transportation charge includes pick-up from points throughout Richmond Hill and Thornhill.
**Age Recommendations:** Ages 8–15.
**Camp Program:** Day camp runs from 9:30 a.m. to 3:00 p.m. Mornings include horse grooming and tacking-up, a one-hour English riding lesson, and experience in cleaning tack, feeding horses, and stable management. Thirty riders per session. Campers bring their own lunch. Cold drinks are available from a machine. Afternoon sessions in horsemanship include learning about horse colours and breeds, equine illnesses, and pony games. Riders must wear a safety helmet with a harness, long pants, and boots with a heel. Family barbecue and demonstration day the last Friday of each session. Bring your own hot dogs and buns; condiments and pop supplied.
**Instructor Qualifications:** Some have CEF certification. The beginners' instructors are more advanced riders in the barn.
**Other Services and Activities:**

- Riding lessons (see listing in Chapter 2).
- One-hour supervised swim.

**Sunnybrook Stables**
P.O. Box 310, Station R
Toronto, ON M4G 4C3
Phone: (416) 444-4044

**Contact:** Anita Barnes.
**Location:** Eglinton and Leslie in Sunnybrook Park. Take the Eglinton bus east from Yonge Street. Get off at Leslie. The walk into the park takes about fifteen minutes.

**Season:** Five two-week sessions between the last week of June and early September. 10:30 a.m. to 3:30 p.m.
**Rates:** Two-week sessions.
**Age Recommendations:** Ages 8–15.
**Camp Program:** Day camp. Includes lunch. English riding. Campers have a morning and afternoon ride. Other activities include lectures on horse care, a visit to the police barn, and other horse-related activities. Up to twenty campers with four instructors.
**Instructor Qualifications:** CEF Level 1 plus.
**Other Services and Activities:**

- Lessons (see listing in Chapter 2).
- Occasional hacking in park for advanced riders.

*Close to Metro Toronto*

**Creditview Stables**
R.R. #10
Brampton, ON L6V 3N2
Phone: (905) 451-8654

**Contact:** Jim Rush.
**Location:** Creditview Road between Steeles and Derry Road.
**Season:** July and August. Monday to Friday, 9:00 a.m. to 4:00 p.m.
**Rates:** Two-week sessions; sign-up through Brampton Parks and Recreation.
**Age Recommendations:** Ages 8–16.
**Camp Program:** Day camp. Campers get two lessons per day as well as classroom instruction in such things as tack parts and cleaning, parts of the horse, horse illnesses, show grooming, showing, and trailering. English. Parents are invited to watch a Friday show. Campers bring their own lunch. Drinks provided. Barbecue once a week. Riders wear helmets, long pants, and boots with a heel. One instructor and counsellors work with riders. Maximum of seven per group.
**Other Services and Activities:**

- Lessons (see listing in Chapter 2).

**Fieldstone Farm**
R.R. #2
Uxbridge, ON L9P 1R2
Phone: (905) 852-6372

**Contact:** Penny McEachern.
**Location:** Twenty minutes east of Highway 404 and north of Davis Drive.
**Season:** One session in July, and two in August.
**Rates:** One-week sessions; fee includes lunch.
**Age Recommendations:** Ages six and up.
**Camp Program:** Day camp. English hunter/jumper. One of the three programs is usually marketed to adults. Of the two for juniors, one concentrates on beginners, the second is for intermediate and advanced riders. Sessions include two lessons per day, lectures, and video coaching. Students discuss their progress and pick up tips for improvement. On the last day, there's a real horse show with an outside judge. Students are expected to bring a change of clothes for nonriding activities. During lessons, they wear helmets and proper footwear. Twelve campers per session in two groups of six. Three instructors.
**Instructor Qualifications:** British Horse Society and twenty-one years experience teaching. The assistants are two students who hold provincial championships in the hunter/jumper field. In 1992, the stable coached four provincial champions in hunter/jumper.
**Other Services and Activities:**

- Lessons (see listing in Chapter 2).
- Camp students receive a reduction on their next month's lessons.
- The viewing lounge is heated and air-conditioned.
- Crafts, games, and swimming.
- Clinics on and off the farm.
- Judges schooling shows.
- CEF carded course designer.

**Five Star Ranch**
3340 Dundas Street West
Oakville, ON L6J 4Z3
Phone: (905) 827-9578

**Contact:** Gail Haynes.
**Location:** Dundas Street just west of Highway 25.
**Season:** July and August. March Break. Christmas Week. Monday to Friday, 8:30 a.m. to 4:30 p.m.
**Rates:** One-week sessions; discount for riders signed up for both the Intro and Level One camps.
**Age Recommendations:** Ages 8–16.
**Camp Program:** Day camp. Western. Riders work at an introductory or more advanced level. Includes education in horseback riding and horse care. Campers receive riding lessons, go on trail rides, experience hands-on horse care sessions, and watch videos on various horse-related subjects. Maximum of twenty campers per session. Ten riders work with one instructor and one assistant.
**Instructor Qualifications:** CEF Level 1 Western coach.
**Other Services and Activities:**

- Trail riding (see listing in Chapter 1) and lessons (see listing in Chapter 2).

**Green Acres Day Camp Inc.**
11123 Kennedy Road
Markham, ON L6C 1P2
Phone: (905) 887-1400

**Contact:** Eddie Bogomlny.
**Location:** On the east side of Kennedy Road three kilometres north of Major Mackenzie. The camp provides door-to-door transportation for certain areas of Metro Toronto.
**Season:** July and August.
**Rates:** Weekly sign-up; half-day riding program in addition to regular day-camp fees.
**Age Recommendations:** Ages 6–16.

**Camp Program:** Day camp with half-day riding option. Minimum of two weeks for riding option. As part of its summer day camp, this camp offers a half-day riding program for beginning to intermediate English riders. Riding is mainly outdoors, with access to an indoor ring in bad weather. Some jumping. Program includes stable management and riding. Students are expected to wear hard-soled shoes and helmets.
**Instructor Qualifications:** The instructors have years of riding experience, both in lessons and as recreational riders. The camp looks for instructors who have rapport with kids as well as knowledge of horses.
**Other Services and Activities:**

- Full day camp program.
- Swimming, farming, variety of sports, other outdoor activities.
- Write for a free brochure.

**Halton School of Equitation Ltd.**
1470 Steeles Avenue
R.R. #2
Hornby, ON L0P 1E0
Phone: (905) 826-2889

**Contact:** Auriel Halliday or Mary Courtney.
**Location:** South side of Steeles, 1.5 kilometres east of Trafalgar Road.
**Season:** Camp runs July and August and during the March Break. Campers are bussed in by the Mississauga YMCA.
**Rates:** Two-week sessions; sign-up through the Mississauga YMCA.
**Age Recommendations:** Ages 7–13.
**Camp Program:** Day camp. English riding. Helmets supplied by the YMCA. About sixty riders are organized into groups of twelve. They rotate through a series of activities for the beginning rider. Day includes riding, horse-related activities, and a games session. During the summer, there is a show on the second Friday of each two-week session. Students demonstrate what they've learned and earn ribbons for achievement. Riders organized into

groups of twelve; six ride in each of the two arenas.
**Other Services and Activities:**

- Lessons (see listing in Chapter 2).

**Harrogate Hills Riding School**
Box 106
Gormley, ON L0H 1G0
Phone: (905) 887-5595

**Contact:** Patricia Gillis.
**Location:** On Stouffville Sideroad, one kilometre west of Highway 404.
**Season:** Camp runs from 9:00 a.m. to 4:00 p.m., Monday to Friday for July and August.
**Rates:** Nine- and ten-day sessions; lower rate for campers who provide their own transportation.
**Age Recommendations:** Ages 7–14. The camp will accept younger children with an interview.
**Camp Program:** Day camp. Lunch provided. English riding. Helmets available. Riders spend most of the day learning horse theory and taking riding instruction. Most children ride horses; two semi-retired ponies are available for younger riders.
**Other Services and Activities:**

- Lessons (see listing in Chapter 2).
- Riders work towards levels of achievement. They receive a certificate at each level.
- Tennis, baseball, and swimming in one of two outdoor pools.

**Hendervale Stables**
5244 #1 Side Road
R.R. #6
Milton, ON L9T 2Y1
Phone: (905) 827-2234

**Contact:** Janet or Heather Manbert.

**Location:** Northwest of the intersection of Highways 25 and 5.
**Season:** Camp runs from 9:00 a.m. to 5:00 p.m., Monday to Friday for July and August. Campers can arrive any time after 7:00 a.m. if their parents work. Assistance with arranging car pools.
**Rates:** One-week sessions; early bookings receive 10 per cent discount; discount for children who attend for four or more weeks.
**Age Recommendations:** Ages 6–16.
**Camp Program:** Day camp. English riding. Riders are assigned their own horse for the day or week. They're responsible for grooming the mount and ride it twice a day. Theory lessons cover such items as the parts of the horse, taking apart and cleaning a bridle, and watching a farrier. During the afternoon, there is also a craft session, treasure hunt, or other horse-related activities. Fridays include a gymkhana or jumping show. Eighteen riders per session. Riders are grouped into three groups of six, according to ability.
**Other Services and Activities:**

- Lessons (see listing in Chapter 2).
- Heated viewing room.
- Lunch room where students can buy a hot dog lunch.

**Park Lane Ranch**
R.R. #2
Tottenham, ON L0G 1W0
Phone: (905) 936-2658

**Contact:** Susan Boyle or Sandra Zelmer.
**Location:** Eight kilometres west of Highway 27 and north of Highway 9.
**Season:** July and August. March Break. Monday to Friday, 10:00 a.m. to 4:00 p.m.
**Rates:** One-week sessions; low rates.
**Age Recommendations:** Ages 6 and up.
**Camp Program:** Day camp. English. Some Western on trail rides. Bring your own lunch. Riders are divided into groups according to their level. They receive a 1½-hour morning lesson

and a $1^{1}/_{2}$-hour afternoon trail ride. Pot luck lunch on Thursdays. Friday is an exhibition and games day to which parents are invited. Riders wear helmets and boots with a heel. Ratio of five riders per instructor.

**Instructor Qualifications:** Owner a CEF Level 1 coach in English. Others have owned and shown horses or come up through the camp programs and worked as trail guides.

**Other Services and Activities:**

- Adventure trail rides (see listing in Chapter 1).
- Will rent Pony Club helmets.

**Pleasure Valley**
2499 Brock Road
R.R. #4
Uxbridge, ON L9P 1R4
Phone: (905) 649-3334

**Contact:** Gary Convery.

**Location:** About three kilometres north of Claremont on the east side of Brock Road.

**Season:** July 1 to Labour Day; camp runs from 9:00 a.m. to 4:00 p.m., Monday to Friday.

**Rates:** One- and two-week sessions; price break on two-week sessions.

**Age Recommendations:** Prefer two groups of six 10- to 15-year-olds per week. Younger children can be placed if there are enough to fill a group.

**Camp Program:** Day camp. Morning and early afternoon sessions include stable work, horse management lessons, and a trail ride. Western riding. Helmets are mandatory. Campers have the use of park facilities from 2:30 p.m. to 4:00 p.m. On Friday, the campers' parents are invited to a noon barbecue and to watch an afternoon competition of all of the campers.

**Other Services and Activities:**

- Trail riding (see listing in Chapter 1).

**The Ranch**
5111 Highway 25
R.R. #1
Milton, ON L9T 2X5
Phone: (905) 876-4511

**Location:** On Highway 25 just south of Milton between the Queen Elizabeth Way and Highway 401.
**Season:** Camp runs from 8:30 a.m. to 4:30 p.m., Monday to Friday for three weeks during July and August.
**Rates:** One-week sessions.
**Age Recommendations:** Ages 8–14.
**Camp Program:** Day camp. Riders spend the whole day around horses. They receive Western riding instruction, help to clean, feed, and groom the horses, go for trail rides and hay rides, and play games with the horses. Riders spend at least two hours per day mounted. Friday features a show in which the campers compete for ribbons. There's a wiener roast. The camp handles ten to twenty children who are divided into two groups depending on their age and ability.
**Other Services and Activities:**

- Trail riding (see listing in Chapter 1) and lessons (see listing in Chapter 2).

**Tanglewood**
164 Cemetery Road
R.R. #1
Uxbridge, ON L9P 1R1
Phone: (905) 852-7180

**Contact:** Kathi Leeson.
**Location:** Southwest corner of Highway 47 and Cemetery Road, just south of Uxbridge. Close to town limits.
**Season:** Camp runs for three weeks during July and August. Monday to Friday, 8:30 a.m. to 4:00 p.m. Maximum of eighteen per session.

**Rates:** One-, two-, and three-week sessions; price break for longer sessions.
**Age Recommendations:** Ages 7–15.
**Camp Program:** Day camp. English riding. Morning activities include a riding lesson, horsemanship session, and a creative arts program. Afternoon sessions include equitation, vaulting, and a further arts session. During equitation sessions, advanced students may try different saddles and styles of riding. Students can work through different vaulting levels. Each week is organized around a theme. The final show is centred around this theme (e.g. a rodeo at the end of Western Week, a vaulting demonstration at the end of Circus Week, etc.). Riders organized into three groups of six with an adult responsible for each group.
**Instructor Qualifications:** CEF Level 1 coach. Certified vaulting instructor.
**Other Services and Activities:**

- Lessons (see listing in Chapter 2).

**Wildwood Manor Ranch**
R.R. #5
Georgetown, ON L7G 4S8
Phone: (905) 877-6852

**Location:** Northeast corner of Trafalgar Road and Highway 7.
**Season:** July and August.
**Rates:** One-week or by-the-day sessions; price break on weekly rate; lower rate for children under the age of eight.
**Age Recommendations:** Ages 3–15.
**Camp Program:** Day camp. Monday to Friday, 9:00 a.m. to 4:30 p.m. Western. Children eight years old and up learn to ride a variety of horses, feed and care for a horse, take care of tack, and how to walk, trot, gallop, and jump a horse. Rodeo every Friday. Riders work for points that earn them free riding time or a chance to show at a Fall Fair. Children under eight have one horseback ride daily, assist with grooming, feeding, and leading young horses, and play games and sports. Six to ten riders with three instructors.

**Instructor Qualifications:** Humber College graduate and a lot of experience riding.

**Other Services and Activities:**

- Trail riding (see listing in Chapter 1) and lessons (see listing in Chapter 2).
- Hayrides, swimming, crafts, and hikes.

## *Southern and Central Ontario*

### Cinch Stables Ltd.

43 Capulet Lane
London, ON N6H 3E6
Phone: (519) 471-3492

**Contact:** Leslie Cornish.

**Location:** South of Highway 27 on Capulet Lane, off Oxford Street in London.

**Season:** July and August. Five sessions per summer, one every second week.

**Rates:** One-week sessions; affordable rates.

**Age Recommendations:** Ages 7–14.

**Camp Program:** Western riding lessons. Trail riding. Horse projects and games. Maximum of sixteen children per session. Riders will pair off in a buddy system that couples young riders with older ones, and experienced riders with less experienced ones. No more than eight riders per lesson. Campers work with three or four instructors at the owner's home farm and a nearby trail riding stable. Children also work on horse projects and games.

**Instructor Qualifications:** First Aid. Instructors are excellent riders who have worked at a trail riding stable. One is a horse owner and competitor. The other is a keen Girl Guide. Both like working with children.

**Other Services and Activities:**

- Adventure trail rides (see listing in Chapter 3).
- Hiking in a nearby provincial park, and swimming in a municipal swimming pool.

**Double DD Ranch**
R.R. #2
Cumberland, ON K0A 1S0
Phone: (613) 833-2317

**Location:** On Highway 17 east between Cumberland and Rockland, about twenty minutes from downtown Ottawa.
**Season:** July and August. Monday to Friday. Includes transportation from Ottawa.
**Rates:** One-week sessions.
**Age Recommendations:** Ages 8–16.
**Camp Program:** Day camp. English and Western. Campers are with the horse all day. They learn the basics of position and control, as well as grooming, horse care, and tacking up. Have private or group lessons and a trail ride each day. Bring lunch Monday to Thursday; on Friday there is a barbecue. Friday mornings are an open house for parents during which the campers demonstrate what they have learned. Helmets are optional and recommended. Riders wear boots with a heel such as rubber rain boots. The camp believes it's important to keep equipment simple so that parents can afford it. Twenty-one campers per week. Work with three instructors. Maximum of seven per instructor.
**Instructor Qualifications:** A lot of riding experience. Community College horsemanship training. Advanced experience in dressage.
**Other Services and Activities:**

- Adventure rides (see listing in Chapter 3).

**Lakeview Stables**
R.R. #3
Port Carling, ON P0B 1J0
Phone: (705) 765-3513

**Contact:** Pam Braybrook.
**Location:** Eight kilometres north of Bala, off Highway 169.

**Season:** July and August. Mondays, Wednesdays, and Fridays, 9:00 a.m. to 4:00 p.m.
**Rates:** By the day.
**Age Recommendations:** Five and up.
**Camp Program:** Day camp. English and Western. Program includes a one-hour lesson in the morning and a trail ride in the afternoon. Ground sessions include stable management, horse and tack knowledge, and general horse care. Bring a lunch. Riders wear long pants and shoes with a heel. Helmets are mandatory. Ratio of five riders per instructor.
**Instructor Qualifications:** A lot of riding and showing since the age of eight.
**Other Services and Activities:**

- Adventure trail rides (see listing in Chapter 3).
- Will supply Pony Club helmets with harness.
- Three schooling shows per year: one Western and two English.

**Ostler Park Equestrian Centre**
R.R. #1
Bobcaygeon, ON K0M 1A0
Phone: (705) 887-1255

**Location:** On County Road 36, just north of Bobcaygeon and Fenelon Falls.
**Season:** July and August. March Break. Christmas week. Monday to Friday, 9:00 a.m. to 4:00 p.m.
**Rates:** One-week sessions; affordable prices.
**Age Recommendations:** Five and up. The average age is six to twelve years old.
**Camp Program:** Day camp. English. Campers ride in the morning and afternoon. The program includes stable management, work on preparing senior students to try for CEF Level 1 coaching, and a demonstration ride for parents at the end of camp. Riders wear Pony Club-approved helmets and boots with a heel. More advanced riders should have breeches and proper

riding boots. Twenty-five campers per week divided into groups according to experience. Five or six campers per instructor.
**Instructor Qualifications:** Pony Club instructor and CEF Level 1 coach. Beginners are taught by senior students under the guidance of the senior instructor.
**Other Services and Activities:**

- Residential camps (see Residential Camp Listings in this chapter).
- Horse shows open to campers and outside students.
- Swimming pool, arts and crafts, and cooperative games.
- Campers can work with young horses and help in the barn.
- Rent helmets by the week.
- Riding program for people with disabilities through the Victoria County Therapeutic Riding Association. This is a Saturday volunteer program for children and adults, run on a seasonal basis.

**Sunrise Stables**
Box 32
Port Severn, ON  L0K 1S0
Phone: (705) 756-2142

**Contact:** Donna Welsh.
**Location:** Off Muskoka Road 34, east of Highway 69.
**Season:** July and August. Three to four days per week, four to five hours per day. Exact times and days by arrangement.
**Rates:** Variable rate depending on amount of time children at facility; willing to custom-design a program for several children.
**Age Recommendations:** Seven and up. Will take five- and six-year-olds if they can sit a pony.
**Camp Program:** Day camp. Camp includes three to four hours of riding, horsemanship, and games. Western. Beginners ride in a fenced area until they can safely control their mounts. They then go for trail rides, including a lunch ride. Emphasis is on safety around horses. Helmets available. Usually three to five riders in a group. Maximum of seven.

**Instructor Qualifications:** A lot of experience riding and running a trail riding stable. The day camp was started because of demand from regular clientele.
**Other Services and Activities:**

- Adventure trail rides (see listing in Chapter 3).

**Thompson's Trail Riding**
R.R. #1
Nobel, ON P0G 1G0
Phone: (705) 342-5844

**Contact:** Ingrid Thompson.
**Location:** On Dillon Road, approximately twenty-four kilometres from Parry Sound, and approximately twelve kilometres from Killbear Provincial Park.
**Season:** July and August. By arrangement.
**Rates:** By the day; 9:00 a.m. to 5:00 p.m.; includes lunch. Lots of personal attention since only two children are handled at one time.
**Age Recommendations:** Eight and up.
**Camp Program:** During the morning, children are introduced to the horse, the stable, the tack, and horse management. They also have a riding lesson. After lunch, children enjoy outdoor recreation and go for a one-hour trail ride. Length of trail depends on the ability and interest of students. English and Western. Approximately eight horses available, including ponies, a part-Arab, a Thoroughbred, a Quarter Horse, and a couple of grades. The main goal of the program is to teach children to enjoy being around horses in a noncompetitive environment. Helmets available and mandatory. Children should wear shoes or boots with a heel, and long pants.
**Instructor Qualifications:** Twenty years of riding and showing.
**Other Activities and Services:**

- Swimming at a public beach, hiking, outdoor adventure.
- Farm animals such as pigs, chickens, and rabbits.

**Walker Stables**
R.R. #2
Holland Centre, ON N0H 1R0
Phone: (519) 794-2375

**Contact:** Jayne Walker.
**Location:** Between Highways 10 and 6, west of Berkeley, east of Dornock, thirty-two kilometres south of Owen Sound.
**Season:** July and August. Camp runs Monday to Friday, 9:00 a.m. to 4:00 p.m. Children bring their own lunch. The camp supplies juice.
**Rates:** One-week program; affordable rates.
**Age Recommendations:** Four and up, including adult beginners. Most riders are between eight and ten years of age.
**Camp Program:** Day camp. Owner and two or three helpers work with up to ten students per week. Concentrate on teaching riders the basics of being safe around horses, learning about the different temperaments horses can have, and learning to share and work with other campers. Camp includes a 1½-hour lesson in the morning, instruction in grooming and tacking horses, and a one- to two-hour trail ride in the afternoon. After an afternoon break, the students may ride in the ring or go for a buggy ride or hay ride. Students may ride several different horses during the week. Instruction is in either Western or English riding. Students can try both, or concentrate on just one style. On Friday, there's a barbecue at lunch. At 3:00 p.m., the riders' parents and friends are invited to see what the children have learned during the week. Helmets are available.
**Other Services and Activities:**

- Farm animals such as cows, foals, and goats.
- Mounted scavenger hunts.

## RESIDENTIAL CAMP LISTINGS

### *Southern Ontario*

**Camp Cherith Ontario**
135 Highland Avenue
Oshawa, ON L1H 6A5
Phone: (905) 579-0123

**Contact:** Beverley Steele.
**Location:** Outside Walkerton.
**Season:** July and August.
**Rates:** One-week sessions; riding option in addition to regular camping fees.
**Age Recommendations:** Children who have graduated from grade four up to seventeen-year-olds.
**Camp Program:** Recreational camp where campers can opt for a horsemanship program. English riding. Basic horsemanship, equitation, trail rides, and some jumping. Gymkhana at the end of each week. Helmets available and mandatory. Forty riders per week. Maximum of five or six riders per group.
**Instructor Qualifications:** Experience with horses and teaching riding.
**Other Services and Activities:**

- Air riflery, canoeing, kayaking, swimming, archery, crafts, nature, bible study, and hiking.

**Cedar Valley Ranch Inc.**
R.R. #1
Cambridge, ON N1R 5S2
Phone: (519) 740-1986

**Contact:** Carol or John Renner.
**Location:** Between Cambridge and Sheffield just off Highway 8.
**Season:** July and August. There is an all-teen week during the last week of June.

**Rates:** Riding camp; one- and two-week sessions.
**Age Recommendations:** Ages 5–15. Children seven and up are preferred for riding.
**Camp Program:** Residential noncompetitive riding camp running from Sunday afternoon to Saturday after lunch. No extra charge for two-week students staying over the weekend. English and Western. Campers in the two-week program can ride English one week, Western the next. Emphasis is on campers learning to ride, learning to respect the horse, and having a good time. Safety is a priority. Campers are assigned a horse and saddle for the week. Mornings include a two-hour lesson. The afternoons are divided between horse care clinics and other activities. Three riding levels at each of English and Western. Riders are expected to bring their oldest clothes, and boots or shoes with a heel but no inside zipper. No more than five campers per counsellor.
**Instructor Qualifications:** Young people with a lot of riding experience and ability who have been through the camp program, can control horses, and enjoy children. The head instructor was the 1987 National Dressage Youth Champion.
**Other Services and Activities:**

- Provides Pony Club helmets. If the helmets are too large, will fit foam under the interior lining to make them fit properly.

**Circle R Ranch**
Box 85
Delaware, ON  N0L 1E0
Phone: (519) 471-3799

**Contact:** Rick Romman.
**Location:** On Delaware Concession 2, which is two kilometres north of Highway 2, eight kilometres west of London.
**Season:** July and August. Includes a series of two-week sessions and one one-week session at the end of August. Sessions are from Sunday to Saturday.

**Rates:** One- and two-week sessions; price break on two-week session.
**Age Recommendations:** Ages 8–15.
**Camp Program:** The idea of the camp program is for children to have fun while they learn to feel comfortable around horses and gain riding basics. To attain this, campers work with horses to learn the basics of grooming, horse care, Western riding, and trail etiquette. They are on or around horses about 3½ hours per day. Campers work in groups of eight according to their age and ability. At least two riding instructors or guides are assigned to each group, depending on the ability of the riders. The final day includes a riding parade to demonstrate to parents and friends what the students have learned during their session.
**Other Services and Activities:**

- Adventure rides (see listing in Chapter 3).
- Write for a free brochure.

**Circle Square Ranch**
R.R. #2
Washago, ON L0K 2B0
Phone: (705) 689-6411

**Contact:** Angie or Frank Wyssen.
**Location:** Just west of Highway 11 near Washago.
**Season:** July and August, one-week sessions from Sunday afternoon to Saturday noon.
**Rates:** One-week sessions.
**Age Recommendations:** Children ages six to eight ride in the ring and may go on one trail ride during the week. Those nine and up spend the first couple of days in the ring but concentrate on trail riding.
**Camp Program:** This is a residential Christian Camp with a riding option. Riders can choose to concentrate on pleasure riding or work towards achievement levels. Vaulting, which is gymnastics on horseback, is also offered. Riders who are working towards achievement levels spend one hour riding, one hour

vaulting, and one hour studying riding theory every day. Riders who just want to pleasure ride spend time helping around the stable and grooming the young horses instead of learning riding theory. Campers are divided into groups of twenty depending on their age and ability. There is usually one riding instructor and a nonriding counsellor per group of eight children. Western. No helmets are available.

**Instructor Qualifications:** The head instructors have years of experience around horses and have been through the learning levels at other riding camps. Their main concern is for the campers to enjoy a safe time around the horses.

**Other Services and Activities:**

- Christian education, devotion, and bible study.
- Swimming, archery, canoeing, outdoor education, and a ropes course.

**Kemur Camp Ltd.**
R.R. #4
Cambridge, ON N1R 5S5
Phone: (519) 621-2109

**Contact:** Christine or Keith Murray.
**Location:** Just off Highway 24, south of Cambridge.
**Season:** Ten weeks during July and August.
**Rates:** Riding camp; one-week sessions; fee includes cost of a camp t-shirt and tack shop credit.
**Age Recommendations:** Ages 6–16.
**Camp Program:** Residential camp for riders who want to spend a lot of time around horses and learn a proper English seat. Campers are with horses most of the day. They ride twice a day and learn stable management in the afternoon. Each child's riding ability is assessed on arrival. Campers are assigned a horse and put into a group according to their experience, size, and skill level. Beginner to advanced. More advanced riders receive coaching in dressage, cross-country, and stadium jumping. Campers also have judging competitions and learn to drive.

Hard hats are mandatory. Riders also need shoes with a heel. Winter boots are not allowed because they are too hot and the zippers mark the saddles. Rubber rain boots or duck boots work well. Loose-fitting jeans for beginners. Breeches or jodhpurs for more advanced. Sixty campers are divided into groups according to riding level. Maximum of seven riders per instructor. Beginners have two instructors per group of seven.

**Instructor Qualifications:** Pony Club experience, most at the B level. Some CEF certification.

**Other Services and Activities:**

- Will loan Pony Club helmets.
- Swimming pool, some crafts and drama, and a sports field.

**Oconto**

59 John Stiver Crescent
Unionville, ON L3R 9B6
Phone: (905) 470-2030

**Contact:** Jennifer Palacios, Bruce Wilson, or Lisa Wilson.

**Location:** Tichborne.

**Season:** July and August.

**Rates:** Camping fee plus a fee for taking the riding option; varied prices depending on the length of the camping session.

**Age Recommendations:** Ages 7–15.

**Camp Program:** Traditional residential camp with riding as an extra option. Campers ride every other day at one of three levels. English only. Campers earn one of five badges based on their basic riding and horsemanship knowledge. Some jumping at advanced levels. Interested campers can also join in morning grooming sessions and evening trail rides. Riders are expected to wear laced boots with a heel, t-shirts, jeans, and their own riding helmet. Maximum of five or six riders with one instructor and one assistant.

**Instructor Qualifications:** Experienced riders with teaching background or who have come up through the camp program. Safety is the first thing they teach.

**Other Services and Activities:**

- Will loan riding helmets with a harness.
- Swimming, sailing, crafts, boardsailing, tripping, canoeing, tennis, archery, nature, kayaking, drama, dance, hiking, and pottery.

**Rocky Ridge Ranch**
R.R. #2
Rockwood, ON N0B 2K0
Phone: (905) 854-2584

**Contact:** Bill Chapman.
**Location:** North of Highway 401, between Highway 25 and Guelph Line.
**Season:** July and August, one-week sessions from Sunday afternoon to Saturday at 3:30 p.m.
**Rates:** One-week sessions; fee reduction if more than one child per family attends.
**Age Recommendations:** Ages 8–18.
**Camp Program:** About 90 per cent of the Rocky Ridge campers are beginning riders. The camp sees itself as providing beginners with basic skills so that they can go on to further riding if they wish. Campers learn the basics of Western riding. They can either simply enjoy being around horses or work towards camp achievement levels. Riders are guaranteed three to five hours around the horses daily. The camp accepts eighty campers per week. There are five to fifteen campers in each riding group, depending on their skill level.
**Instructor Qualifications:** The camp is headed by a Western rider with certification from an American association that handles riding camp supervision. Other staff have come through the Rocky Ridge Ranch camp program; most have additional training.
**Other Activities and Services:**

- Trail rides (see listing in Chapter 1) and adventure trail rides (see listing in Chapter 3).

Royal Lifesaving swimming programs.
ual and group sports organized by staff.

Caledon, ON 1C0
Phone: (519) 941-4501

**Contact:** Peter or Rebecca Bruce.
**Location:** Three kilometres south of Orangeville on Highway 10.
**Season:** Last week of June to first week of September.
**Rates:** Weekly fee for riding program; higher rate for advanced English riding program; price break on two-week sessions; riding is part of the hockey and golf programs.
**Age Recommendations:** Ages 9–19. The camp is divided by age groups with sessions concentrating on groups 14–16, 12–14, and 9–13.
**Camp Program:** Residential sports camp with riding. English and Western. The specialized riding program includes a Western or English lesson in the morning, theory, and an afternoon trail ride. Riders can also choose to study vaulting, horse science, or leathercraft. The generalized program includes an afternoon trail ride. Riders are expected to bring long pants and shoes or boots with a heel. Group size varies from six to eight riders. Group maximum is eight.
**Instructor Qualifications:** Camp Horsemanship Association certification. This certification is offered by an American group that offers coaching levels similar to those used by the Canadian Equestrian Federation.
**Other Services and Activities:**

- Provide Pony Club helmets for all campers.
- Other programs include a hockey school, tennis, and golf camps, plus a special camp for ten- to thirteen-year-olds, during which they live in teepees, canoe, learn archery, and cook outdoors. These groups ride in the afternoon.

**Wahanowin**
62 Heath Street West
Toronto, ON M4V 1T4
Phone: (416) 975-1916

**Contact:** Bruce Nashman.
**Location:** Near Orillia on Lake Couchiching.
**Season:** July and August. The music camp in August and early September also includes riding.
**Rates:** Residential riding camp; one-, two-, three-, four-, and seven-week sessions; one ten-day session.
**Age Recommendations:** Ages 6–15.
**Camp Program:** Residential co-ed general summer camp. English riding is part of the program as well as an option. Enthusiastic riders can increase their riding time by adopting a horse for the day, trail riding, and riding during the open period before dinner. Mainly beginner and intermediate level. Some advanced. Riders work through basic riding levels. Some dressage. One or two riding shows per summer. Campers are advised to bring boots with a heel. The camp supplies Pony Club and hockey helmets. Two or three riding staff work with eight to ten children and their counsellors in each riding session.
**Instructor Qualifications:** Experience with riding, teaching, and animal care. Two are of university age.
**Other Services and Activities:**

- Swimming, water skiing, sports, theatre, sailing, tennis, gymnastics, ropes course, canoeing, creative arts, and rock climbing.

**Waterbrook Farm Camp**
R.R. #1
Hagersville, ON N0A 1H0
Phone: (905) 768-1486

**Contact:** Janette Matheson.
**Location:** Hagersville, fifty kilometres south of Hamilton.

**Season:** July and August.
**Rates:** Payment by the week; very affordable rates.
**Age Recommendations:** Ages 7–13. Some six-year-olds. Campers between fourteen and fifteen years old are counsellors-in-training.
**Camp Program:** Residential Christian camp. Runs weekly, Sunday night to Saturday morning. English and Western. Riders are put on a different horse each day. They work at one of five levels. The first level introduces them to the basics of horsemanship in a small fenced paddock. At the second level, they move to a larger paddock, learn how to rein a horse, and how to post. At the third level, they learn basic control and how to canter. Campers who have passed the third level go on trail rides in the afternoon. Others may work on grooming, longeing, and basic horse care. Campers get one half-hour riding lesson and half an hour of animal husbandry each day. There's a horse show every Friday. Children are divided into groups of four and compete at their own level. Every child gets a ribbon. Riders are expected to wear boots with a heel and a hockey, bike, or riding helmet with a chin harness. There's a ratio of one instructor or counsellor-in-training for each rider.
**Instructor Qualifications:** An outside instructor with CEF certification comes in to give occasional lessons. Other instructors are people who have been through the camp program.
**Other Services and Activities:**

- Hockey and Pony Club helmets can be loaned to riders.
- Bible studies, crafts, care of farm animals, campfires, photography, swimming, and hay rides.

**Western Kids Camp**
R.R. #3
Strathroy, ON N7G 3H5
Phone: 247-3644

**Contact:** Fred and Gail Cahill.
**Location:** Six kilometres south of Highway 402, west of Strathroy.

**Season:** July and August.
**Rates:** By the week.
**Age Recommendations:** Ages 8–13. One teen week in August for fourteen- to seventeen-year-olds.
**Camp Program:** Western riding camp. Campers live on a southern Ontario ranch where they sleep in covered wagons and experience the life of a real cowhand. Campers feed the livestock, including calves and horses, daily. They learn riding, roping, and horsemanship, plus explore the banks of the Sydenham River on horseback. Forty children per week. Campers are divided into groups of six. There are eight riding instructors. The camp's priorities are to provide children with a new and different environment, to make them comfortable around horses, and to teach safety around horses.
**Instructor Qualifications:** First Aid. CPR. The owners have a working cattle ranch, and have worked cattle from horseback for twenty-five years. Staff have experience working with children. Most have either worked cattle from horseback or trail-ridden.
**Other Services and Activities:**

- Volleyball, baseball, and crafts.
- Work towards swimming badges in a Texas-sized pool.

*Central Ontario*

**The Easter Seal Society of Ontario**
250 Ferrand Drive, Suite 200
Don Mills, ON M3C 3P2
Phone: (416) 421-8377 or 1-800-668-6252

**Contact:** Mark Sack.
**Location:** Kirkland Lake.
**Season:** July and August.
**Rates:** Residential camp for those with physical disabilities; fee is based on ability to pay; Easter Seal Society and various service clubs assist with fees.
**Age Recommendations:** Ages 6–18.

**Camp Program:** Residential recreational camp for children with disabilities. Riding is part of the program. Campers get an opportunity to ride a horse in a ring. The purpose of such activity is to give campers a new experience and help to raise their self-confidence. Campers also receive lessons in grooming and horse care. Western saddles. Helmets provided and mandatory. Campers ride two at a time. Each horse has a leader and two side-walkers. There is one instructor per rider.
**Instructor Qualifications:** Students from the three-year Equine Studies program at New Liskeard Agricultural College.
**Other Services and Activities:**

- Swimming, canoeing, sailing, music, campcraft, creative arts, sports, fishing, drama, computers, canoe tripping, and lifeskills.

**Frontier Trails Kids Kamp**
R.R. #6
Eganville, ON  K0J 1T0
Phone: (613) 625-2416

**Contact:** Marie Tubby.
**Location:** Eganville.
**Season:** Weekends, March Break week, July and August.
**Rates:** Variable rates depending on the amount of riding.
**Age Recommendations:** Ages 6–16, depending on the week.
**Camp Program:** Campers can opt for riding as part of a full-time activity program. This allows a half-hour to one hour of riding per day. The full riding option is two hours of riding per day. More experienced campers can go on an overnight trail ride. Western and English; mostly Western unless the riders are experienced. Boots and helmets are required and can be rented for the session. There are three to ten riders per group, depending on the type of program and number of interested campers.
**Instructor Qualifications:** Depends on the year.
**Other Services and Activities:**

- Archery, mountain biking, trampoline, swimming to Red

Cross badges, crafts, camp-outs, Huck Finn rafting, fort building, and canoeing.

**Gay Venture**
87 Inglewood Drive
Toronto, ON  M4T 1H4
Phone: (416) 481-7322

**Contact:** Janet Adamson.
**Location:** Haliburton.
**Season:** July and August.
**Rates:** Girls' residential camp with riding option; four-week rate.
**Age Recommendations:** Ages 10–15.
**Camp Program:** Residential camp with riding option. Option limited to campers at Gay Venture for one month or more.
**Other Services and Activities:**

- Swimming, canoeing, drama, pioneer crafts, environmental awareness, land sports, water skiing, canoe tripping, tennis, windsurfing, kayaking, sailing, crafts, archery, pottery, ropes course, and paddle making.

**Glen Bernard**
206 Lord Seaton Road
Willowdale, ON  M2P 1K9
Phone: (416) 225-4166

**Contact:** Jocelyn Palm.
**Location:** Sundridge.
**Season:** July and August.
**Rates:** Residential camp with riding option; additional fee for riding for two or three weeks.
**Age Recommendations:** Ages 7–16.
**Camp Program:** Residential sports camp for girls. Riding is an option. English only. Campers are put in a group at their own level. They learn a variety of skills and earn badges according to

their horse knowledge and riding ability. Includes ring and trail riding. Jumping, dressage, and driving are taught at the higher levels. Riders are expected to have shoes or boots with a heel, long pants, and a helmet. No more than four or five campers per instructor.

**Instructor Qualifications:** Varies. Some have a lot of riding experience, others have CEF coaching levels.

**Other Services and Activities:**

- Provides Pony Club helmets.
- Sailing, kayaking, crafts, life-saving skills, ropes course, board-sailing, theatre, canoeing, trampoline, canoe tripping, tennis, swimming, archery, and Earth education.

**The Horse People Inc.**
R.R. #1
Wendover, ON K0A 3K0
Phone: (613) 673-5905

**Contact:** Bev or Wolf Schinke.

**Location:** Wendover.

**Season:** Year-round, including camps during March Break, Christmas Week, Easter, and July and August.

**Rates:** Residential riding camp; two-, four-, six-, and eight-week sessions; special eight-week competitor program at additional cost.

**Age Recommendations:** Ages 9–18 for summer camp. Adults are welcome and participate in programs.

**Camp Program:** Residential riding camp. Complete horsemanship program with instruction in dressage, jumping, cross-country, and steeplechase. English lessons. ASTM-approved helmets and riding boots are mandatory. Junior beginning riders may wear track pants or other comfortable pants. Others should have breeches or jodhpurs. Campers work in groups of five or six, depending on the level of riders.

**Instructor Qualifications:** CEF Level 1 coaching certificate.

**Other Services and Activities:**

- Swimming pool, lounge, trails, and recreation hall.

- Will provide accommodation for horse and rider being coached.
- Three to four day clinics throughout year.
- Write for a free brochure.

**Lakefield Camp International**
980 Yonge Street, Suite 200
Toronto, ON M4W 2J5
Phone: (416) 323-9090

**Contact:** For horse information only: Pat Life or Amy Croteau at Kawartha Equine Centre, (705) 295-6668.
**Location:** Lakefield.
**Season:** July and August.
**Rates:** English as a Second Language Camp with riding option; July sign-up for six, twelve, or eighteen lessons; August sign-up for five, ten, or fifteen lessons; lesson fee in addition to regular camp fees; camp has two-, three-, and four-week sessions.
**Age Recommendations:** Ages 8–16.
**Camp Program:** Residential camp with riding option. Riders are transported to a nearby equestrian centre for lessons at a variety of levels. English riding. Beginners start on the longe. Depending on their ability, other riders may do a number of equine activities including hacking, working in the hunter/jumper ring, cross-country jumping, etc. Riders wear ASTM-approved helmets and boots with a heel. Maximum of four riders per instructor.
**Instructor Qualifications:** CEF Level 1 coaching certificate.
**Other Services and Activities:**

- Will supply ASTM-approved helmets.
- Theatre arts, team sports, kayaking, canoeing, dance, drawing, painting, sailing, swimming, computers, windsurfing, and martial arts.

**Manitou-Wabing Sports and Arts Centre**
251 Davenport Road
Toronto, ON M5R 1J9
Phone: (416) 922-2447

**Location:** McKellar.
**Season:** July and August.
**Rates:** Sports and art camp with riding option; riding fees in addition to regular camp fees; can arrange for riding once a day, twice a day, or three times a week.
**Age Recommendations:** Ages 8–17.
**Camp Program:** Residential sports and arts camp with riding option. English. Lessons include equitation, hunter/jumper, and trail. Shows for campers. Helmets, boots, and breeches or jodhpurs are recommended. Up to fourteen riders per group with six instructors.
**Instructor Qualifications:** British Horse Society certification.
**Other Services and Activities:**

- Tennis, baseball, visual arts, theatre, waterskiing, basketball, dance, broadcasting, etc.

**New Frenda Youth Camp**
Box 520
Oshawa, ON L1H 7M1
Phone: (905) 579-9538

**Contact:** Milton Perkins. During the camping season, contact the Director of Horsemanship Program at (705) 765-5597.
**Location:** On Muskoka Road 7, southeast of Rosseau.
**Season:** Late June to the end of August.
**Rates:** Residential camp with riding option and riding for general campers; additional fee for riding option.
**Age Recommendations:** Ages 8–16.
**Camp Program:** Residential outdoor camp with riding options. The generalized riding program includes one ride per day, and concentrates on pleasure riding. The specialized riding program

is available only during two-week sessions. Riders spend two periods a day around horses. They learn to ride and care for their mounts. English and Western. Includes three levels: beginner, intermediate, and advanced. Riders are expected to have high riding boots that cover the ankle and have a heel. Group size varies from six and up, depending on what is being done. Group maximum is seven or eight per instructor.

**Instructor Qualifications:** Certified by Ontario Horsemanship Association.

**Other Services and Activities:**

- Will loan riding helmets with a harness.
- Windsurfing, sailing, nature, canoeing, archery, photo, arts and crafts, swimming, and water skiing.

**Onondaga Camp**
950 Yonge Street, Suite 200
Toronto, ON M4W 2J4
Phone: (416) 323-0111

**Contact:** Horsemanship Director or anyone who answers the phone.

**Location:** Minden.

**Season:** End of June to September 3.

**Rates:** Residential camp with riding; sign-up by month or two-week session; special low rates on last two weeks of August.

**Age Recommendations:** Ages 6–15.

**Camp Program:** Residential general activities camp. Includes ring and trail riding. Done on a sign-up basis. Campers are expected to wear helmets and boots with a heel. Two instructors and two counsellors-in-training work with the riders.

**Other Services and Activities:**

- Scuba diving, canoe tripping, windsurfing, arts and crafts, karate, sailing, water skiing, parasailing, kayaking, archery, drama, ecology, canoeing, mountain biking, tennis, flying fox, dance, crossbow, swimming, and sports.

**Ostler Park Equestrian Centre**
R.R. #1
Bobcaygeon, ON  K0M 1A0
Phone: (705) 887-1255

**Location:** On County Road 36 just north of Bobcaygeon and Fenelon Falls.
**Season:** July and August. March Break. Christmas week.
**Rates:** Riding camp; sign-up by the week.
**Age Recommendations:** Ages five and up. The average age is nine to fifteen years old.
**Camp Program:** Residential camp. Sessions run from Sunday to the following Saturday. English. Campers ride in the afternoon and evening. The program includes stable management, work on preparing senior students to try for CEF Coaching Level 1, and a demonstration ride for parents at the end of camp. Riders wear Pony Club-approved helmets and boots with a heel. More advanced riders should have breeches and proper riding boots. Twenty-five campers per week divided into groups according to experience. Five or six campers per instructor.
**Instructor Qualifications:** Pony Club instructor and CEF Level 1 coach. Beginners are taught by senior students under the guidance of the senior instructor.
**Other Services and Activities:**

- Day camps (see Day Camp Listings in this chapter).
- Swimming pool, arts and crafts, and cooperative games.
- Campers can work with young horses and help in the barn.
- Rent helmets by the week.

**Otterdale**
1632B Bayview Avenue
Toronto, ON  M4G 3B7
Phone: (416) 322-6500

**Contact:** Michael Southam.
**Location:** Lombardy, between Ottawa and Kingston.

**Season:** July and August.
**Rates:** Residential camp with riding; one- to three-week sessions; price break on longer sessions.
**Age Recommendations:** Ages 7–16.
**Camp Program:** Residential general camp with pleasure riding included as an activity. English. Some Western if requested. Campers learn how to groom, saddle, and bridle a horse. They learn the basics of riding in an enclosed ring before heading out on the trail. The emphasis is on having fun on horseback. Campers work through three levels depending on their age and experience. Certificates at each level. Three instructors handle groups of twelve to fourteen riders.
**Instructor Qualifications:** Pony Club experience or horsemanship graduates from Humber or Seneca College. The camp looks for staff who are safety-conscious, interested in younger children, and enthusiastic.
**Other Services and Activities:**

- Tennis, kayaking, archery, movie making, orienteering, sailing, swimming, rappelling, field games, music, basketball, canoeing, windsurfing, crafts, crossbows, and skin diving.

**The Peterson Woods Outdoor Centre**
Box 730
Minden, ON K0M 2K0
Phone: (705) 286-3555

**Contact:** Jim McHardy.
**Location:** Minden.
**Season:** July and August. Adults can attend some August and fall sessions.
**Rates:** Residential camping with riding as part of program; five-day session in July; low rates.
**Age Recommendations:** Ages eight and up.
**Camp Program:** This is a residential general camp. July sessions are for children with emotional or behavioral problems who are receiving support from child and family services, the Children's

Aid Society, school board personnel, or private therapists. Campers must be referred. English riding. Riding is done in conjunction with the full program, which introduces campers to a number of outdoor activities. It is used to help campers enhance their own self-image, and as part of a social skills program in which groups work together. Campers are expected to have hard-soled shoes and long pants. Pony Club helmets are supplied. Group size varies from one staff with two children, to two staff with eight to ten adults, depending on need.
**Instructor Qualifications:** Riding and coaching experience.
**Other Services and Activities:**

- Work with adult mental health and young offender clients in August.

**Ponacka**
R.R. #4
Peterborough, ON K9J 6X5
Phone: (705) 748-9470

**Location:** Highland Grove.
**Season:** July and August.
**Rates:** Resident campers sign up for riding lessons in series of five, ten, or fifteen lessons.
**Age Recommendations:** Ages 8–15.
**Camp Program:** Traditional residential camp where campers stay in tents or cabins without hydro. English riding lessons are an option. Beginner to advanced. Riders are evaluated on arrival. Riding campers also go for trail rides and day-long rides. Campers work towards awards that structure their learning and include knowledge in stable management, riding, and theory. The emphasis is on having fun and being safe around horses, horse care, and horsemanship. Riders are expected to wear decent boots. The camp provides helmets with a harness. Two instructors work with seven to eight campers per lesson.
**Instructor Qualifications:** University students with extensive riding experience. Most have worked at, or managed, stables.

**Other Services and Activities:**

- Nature, canoeing, bushcraft, swimming, sailing, lapidary, kayaking, windsurfing, crafts, woodwork, and waterskiing.

**Taylor Statten Camp**
59 Hoyle Avenue
Toronto, ON M4S 2X5
Phone: (416) 486-6959

**Location:** Algonquin Park.
**Season:** July and August.
**Rates:** Residential camp with small amount of riding; regular camping fees for half and full session; different rates for fifteen-day session and special twelve-day session for children ages 7-9.
**Age Recommendations:** Ages 7–16.
**Camp Program:** Residential private camp with riding included in the regular program. Campers gets basic instruction in English riding. More advanced riders receive instruction in equestrian skills such as dressage. Campers ride four or five times per month. Riders are expected to wear boots with a heel and a riding helmet. The rider:instructor ratio is usually about 3:1.
**Instructor Qualifications:** Experienced instructors.
**Other Services and Activities:**

- Canoe tripping, sailing, drama, windsurfing, swimming, tennis, music, canoeing, crafts, archery, and ecology.

**White Pine**
40 Lawrence Avenue West
Toronto, ON M5M 1A4
Phone: (416) 322-6250

**Contact:** Adam or Joe Kronick.
**Location:** Haliburton.
**Season:** July and August.
**Rates:** Residential camp with riding as part of program; special

rates for campers who stay the complete season.
**Age Recommendations:** Ages 8–16. Participation in activities such as jumping and the musical ride depend on the camper's ability to control a horse.
**Camp Program:** Residential camp with five major emphases: riding, canoe tripping, tennis, aquatics, and creative arts. English riding with some Western. Cabin groups ride one or two times a week. Interested campers may opt for a number of activities including: adopt-a-horse—includes early morning rides and grooming; riding club—includes learning dressage, a musical ride, and jumping shows; and trail rides—includes overnight rides.

Morning and afternoon periods are also open for specialized riding instruction. Riders are expected to wear rubber boots, riding boots, or shoes with a heel, and a pair of jeans. The camp provides helmets with an attached chin strap. Helmets are sprayed after each use. Six full-time instructors. Two go with a trail ride of eight to ten campers. Maximum lesson size of one instructor per four riders.
**Instructor Qualifications:** Pony Club trained. Most have a lot of experience riding and working around horses.
**Other Services and Activities:**

- Gymnastics, water skiing, sailing, windsurfing, drama, etc.

# Glossary

**Appaloosa:** Breed of horse originally bred by the Nez Percé Indians of the United States. Many have a spotted coat and striped hooves.

**Arab:** Breed of horse from Arabia. These horses tend to have a lot of stamina. Can be high-spirited. Not usually thought of as a beginner's horse.

**assessment lesson:** When beginning to take lessons at a new stable, experienced riders usually have an assessment lesson to give the head instructor an opportunity to evaluate their riding level. This allows the instructor to put new riders into a group working at, or close to, their level.

**bridle:** Piece of tack worn on the horse's head. A bit in the horse's mouth allows the rider to control the horse's direction and speed.

**canter:** Word for a slow run. *Also see* lope.

**crop:** A short whip used to reinforce directions from the rider.

**cross:** Refers to a mixing of two horse breeds e.g. a Thoroughbred/Arab cross.

**cross-country:** Usually refers to a series of jumps set up around a field or along a wooded trail.

**double:** Refers to having two riders mounted on the same horse, usually a child and an adult. This is not a safe way to ride.

**draft:** A heavy horse formerly used to pull farm equipment. Many draft horses are crossed with lighter saddle horses to produce a heavy horse that can be ridden by large riders.

**dressage:** Careful training of the horse and rider so that the horse responds to subtle signals from the rider.

**equitation:** Term for the correct method of sitting on a horse and proper use of the natural aids.

**evaluation lesson.** *See* assessment lesson.

**farrier:** Blacksmith who trims the horse's feet and fits it with shoes.

**grade:** A horse of no particular breed.

**grooming:** Brushing the horse.

**gymkhana:** Series of games on horseback.

**hacking:** British term used to refer to riding on the trails.

**half board.** *See* part board.

**horse leasing:** Some stables have horses they will lease to interested riders for a monthly fee as well as the expenses of maintaining the horse. This is a useful introduction to horse ownership for people who can afford to keep a horse but don't have enough money to buy one.

**hunter/jumper:** Refers to stables interested in providing training for those interested in learning how to jump.

**introductory lesson:** Some stables have a lesson or series of lessons that introduce the nonrider to horsemanship.

**judging competition:** Competition during which contestants place the horses and riders in a mock show. Points are given for explanations of why horses and riders were placed where they were.

**length of lesson:** Many stables have lessons that are one hour in length. In other cases, instructors gauge the end of the lesson according to what the horse or rider has accomplished. Such stables may provide lessons that are longer or shorter than the norm.

**longe line:** A long line that a handler can use to control the horse as it moves in a circle around the handler. Many instructors control the horse in this way while they teach beginning riders the basics of balance.

**lope:** Western term for a canter or slow run.

**make-up lesson:** A lesson that can be taken, at no extra cost, if a rider misses a scheduled lesson.

**musical ride:** Series of moves on horseback performed to music. This assists riders in learning precision and control.

**Paint:** A white horse with large brown or black patches.

**Palomino:** A golden coloured horse with blonde mane and tail.

**part board:** Some lesson stables allow regular students to pay half the board on a lesson horse in exchange for the use of that horse at prescribed times. Other stables will make arrangements for students to share the boarding costs with an individual owner who can't quite afford the cost of board.

**Pinto:** A horse with colouring similar to that of a Paint.

**pleasure riding:** Riding for the pure enjoyment of it, rather than working towards competition.

**police barn:** Stable where the horses used by Metro Toronto's mounted unit are housed.

**Pony Club:** This is a nonprofit group that provides riding instruction and showing opportunities for young riders. It is an excellent introduction to the sport of riding.

**posting:** When a horse trots, the rider bounces up out of the saddle. Riders who "post" control the amount of bounce by rising in the stirrups as they feel themselves moving up. They then sit back down in the saddle. This controlled rising and sitting with the movement of the horse is called posting.

**practice session:** Period during which some lesson stables will allow students to rent a horse to practice skills learned in their regular lessons.

**Quarter Horse:** Breed of horse developed in the United States as a short-distance runner and later used as a cattle horse. Tend to be quiet and forgiving of rider errors. Frequently used for beginning riders.

**Quarter Horse type:** Similar to a Quarter Horse but without registration papers.

**riding crop.** *See* crop.

**stirrup:** An attachment hanging from the saddle to support the rider's foot.

**tack:** Bridle, saddle, and other paraphernalia worn by the horse.

**Thoroughbred:** Horse with racehorse breeding. Usually used by English riders. Tend to be large and rather high-spirited. Not usually recommended for beginners.

**Thoroughbred type:** Similar to Thoroughbred but without registration papers.

**trail etiquette:** Refers to the rules for riding on the trail. Rules include keeping several horse lengths behind the horse in front and not passing the lead horse.

**Trillium circuit:** A provincial competitive circuit with classes in hunter, jumper, and dressage.

**vaulting:** Gymnastics on horseback designed to improve riders balance.

# Index

# J



# K



# L



# M



# N



# O



# P



# Q



# R

# About the Author

LIKE MANY TORONTO RESIDENTS, Helen Mason was a teenager before she mounted anything more lively than a carousel horse. Since then, she has written horse-related articles that have appeared in equine magazines in Canada and the United States, and in general interest publications in Hong Kong, Singapore, and Canada. She has also written two horse training manuals for the Independent Study Division of the University of Guelph.

Helen lives in the country outside Parry Sound with her husband, son, dog, cat, and pet rat. "Since I bought my first mount with the paycheque from my first full-time job, horses have been an important part of my life," she claims. "I travel in search of them, write about them, and generally enjoy the sight, sound, and smell of them." Helen currently owns a twenty-one-year-old American Saddlebred gelding named The Bold One and an eleven-year-old Appaloosa gelding named Apple. Her son rides Tiffany, a thirteen-year-old pony mare.

Photo Credit: John Mason